Human Rights,
International Law
and the Helsinki Accord

Human Rights, International Law and the Helsinki Accord

edited by
THOMAS BUERGENTHAL
assisted by
JUDITH R. HALL

Published under the auspices of
The American Society of International Law

LandMark Studies
ALLANHELD, OSMUN/UNIVERSE BOOKS
Montclair/New York

ALLANHELD, OSMUN & CO. PUBLISHERS, INC.
Montclair, New Jersey

Published in the United States of America in 1977
by Allanheld, Osmun & Co., 19 Brunswick Road, Montclair, N.J. 07042
and by Universe Books, 381 Park Avenue South, N.Y., N.Y. 10016
Distribution: Universe Books

LIBRARY OF CONGRESS CATALOGING IN PUBLICATION DATA

Main entry under title:

Human rights, international law and the Helsinki Accord.

   Includes index.
   1. Civil rights (International law)   I. Buergenthal, Thomas.
K3240.4.H84   341.48'1   77-11762
ISBN 0-87663-828-0

Printed in the United States of America

Preface

After the conclusion in 1975 of the Helsinki Conference on Security and Cooperation in Europe, some American human rights specialists urged the American Society of International Law to seek funds for an international meeting of academic international lawyers and human rights specialists to explore the human rights implications of the Helsinki Final Act. Their assumption was that the Final Act was too important an instrument to be left entirely in the hands of politicians, government officials and special interest groups. They were particularly afraid that, given the realities of political life, too little careful thought would be given to the long-term legal significance and evolutionary potential of this instrument. They were convinced, moreover, that the gradual transformation of the Final Act into a realistic blueprint for future action could be greatly assisted by a multinational rather than purely national scholarly discussion on exploring the meaning and legal significance of the Final Act.

This suggestion was incorporated into a proposal by the Society to the Ford Foundation, which resulted in a grant to the Society for a project on the Helsinki Final Act as part of a broad program of research and study in the field of the international protection of human rights, for which the Society is deeply grateful. Given the timing of the planned 1977 Belgrade Review Conference, it seemed appropriate to make this project the first part of the program. The project centered around a conference held in June 1977 in collaboration with the Faculty of Law and Political Science of the University of Strasbourg, which provided most gracious facilities and hospitality. The chapters contained in this volume were initially presented and critically examined at that meeting.

Special thanks are due to the Faculty of Law and Political Science and to the following individuals for their energetic and generous efforts in helping to make the conference a success: Professor Heribert Golsong, Director of Legal Affairs of the Council of Europe; Dean Gérard Cohen Jonathan of the Strasbourg Law Faculty; and to Professor Thomas Buergenthal of the University of Texas School of Law. Professor Buergenthal chaired the steering group that planned and organized the project, and has edited the present volume. That steering group consisted of Suzanne Bastid, University of Paris; Antonio Cassese, University of Florence; James Fawcett, University of London; Heribert Golsong; John Lawrence Hargrove; Louis Henkin, Columbia University; H.G. Schermers, University of Amsterdam, and Louis B. Sohn, Harvard University. These individuals, with the exception of Professor Fawcett, who was prevented by family illness from participating, joined the following persons who met as a working group in Strasbourg: Bengt Broms, University of Helsinki; Gérard Cohen Jonathan; Jan de Meyer, University of Louvain; Pierre Dupuy, University of Strasbourg; C. Clyde Ferguson, Harvard University; Jochen A. Frowein, University of Bielefeld; Rosalyn Higgins, London School of Economics; Jean Paul Jacqué, University of Strasbourg; Wilhelm A. Kewenig, University of Kiel; Charles-Alexandre Kiss, University of Strasbourg; Virginia Leary, State University of New York at Buffalo; Roger Pinto, University of Paris; John P. Salzberg and James Schollaert of the staff of the International Relations Committee of the U.S. House of Representatives; Walter Tornopolski, York University; and Karel Vasak, Division of Human Rights and Peace, UNESCO.

The views expressed herein are not necessarily those of the institutions with which the authors or other participants may be associated, nor of the American Society of International Law, which as an organization characteristically does not take positions on matters of public concern.

> John Lawrence Hargrove
> Director of Studies
> American Society of
> International Law

Washington, D.C.
August, 1977

Contents

*Human Rights,
International Law
and the Helsinki Accord*

1 International Human Rights Law and the Helsinki Final Act: Conclusions

by THOMAS BUERGENTHAL

INTRODUCTION

The Final Act of the Conference on Security and Cooperation in Europe (CSCE) was signed in Helsinki, Finland, on August 1, 1975, by 33 European nations as well as the United States and Canada. The signatories reflect the broad spectrum of political opinion and ideological orientation in the Europe of today. They include the member states of the Warsaw Pact and NATO, as well as various neutral and nonaligned countries. The only European state not to attend the conference was Albania.

Drafted in a number of negotiating stages over a period of three years, the Helsinki Final Act* is a massive instrument formulated in treaty language without being a treaty. It addresses a wide range of topics reflecting the political, military, economic, humanitarian, cultural, and educational concerns of the participating states. In addition to the preambular material, the Final Act consists of three principal parts, popularly referred to as "Baskets," and a follow-up section.

Part I of the Final Act, entitled "Questions Relating to Security in Europe," deals with confidence-building measures, security, and disarmament. This section also contains the "Declaration on Principles Guiding Relations between Par-

---

*Sometimes referred to colloquially as the Helsinki Accord(s) or the Helsinki Declaration. Strictly speaking, the latter refers only to that part of the Final Act entitled, "Declaration on Guiding Principles."

ticipating States.'' The declaration proclaims 10 guiding principles. These are characterized in the Final Act as being ''of primary significance'' and as having to be ''equally and unreservedly applied, each of them being interpreted taking into account the other.'' The guiding principles deal with sovereign equality, use of force, inviolability of frontiers, territorial integrity, peaceful settlement of disputes, nonintervention in internal affairs, human rights, self-determination, cooperation among states, and the fulfillment in good faith of international law obligations. Policies relating to cooperation in the fields of economics, science, technology and environment are dealt with in part II of the Final Act, which also contains a section on ''Questions Relating to Security and Cooperation in the Mediterranean.''

Basket III of the Helsinki Final Act is entitled ''Cooperation in Humanitarian and Other Fields.'' The principal topics subsumed under this heading are human contacts, information, cultural cooperation and exchanges, and educational cooperation and exchanges. Basket III, together with various clauses of the declaration on guiding principles, contains the human rights undertakings that the Helsinki Final Act proclaims.* This book explores the major international human rights issues raised by these provisions.

The Helsinki Final Act concludes with a section on ''Follow Up to the Conference.'' In it, the signatory states ''declare their resolve'' to implement the provisions of this instrument through unilateral, bilateral, and multilateral action, including meetings of experts from the participating states. Paragraphs 2 and 3 of this section read as follows:

2. *Declare furthermore their resolve* to continue the multilateral process initiated by the Conference:

(a) by proceeding to a thorough exchange of views both on the implementation of the provisions of the Final Act and of the tasks defined by the Conference, as well as, in the context of the questions dealt with by the latter, on the deepening of their mutual relations, the improvement of security and the development of co-operation in Europe, and the development of the process of détente in the future;

*These texts are reproduced in the Appendix to this book.

(b) by organizing to these ends meetings among their representatives, beginning with a meeting at the level of representatives appointed by the Ministers of Foreign Affairs. This meeting will define the appropriate modalities for the holding of other meetings which could include further similar meetings and the possibility of a new Conference;

3. The first of the meetings indicated above will be held at Belgrade in 1977. A preparatory meeting to organize this meeting will be held at Belgrade on 15 June 1977. The preparatory meeting will decide on the date, duration, agenda and other modalities of the meeting of representatives appointed by the Ministers of Foreign Affairs;

The preparatory Belgrade conference, which adjourned shortly before this book went to press (August 1977), was part of the follow-up process envisaged by the Final Act.

The desire to assist in this follow-up and implementation process prompted the convening of the conference of American and Western European international lawyers that met in Strasbourg, France, in June 1977, to explore the international legal meaning and implications of the human rights provisions of the Final Act. To this end, a series of papers by leading scholars were commissioned and discussed at the meeting. The papers were revised by the authors after the meeting to enable them to take account of and respond to the issues and arguments that were raised by the conference participants. The revised papers are chapters 2 through 7 of this book. The final report presented to and discussed at the Strasbourg meeting was a summary of the overall conclusions that emerged from the discussion of the individual papers. This summary was prepared by me and is reproduced, with minor revisions based on suggestions by the conference participants, in the pages that follow.*

CONFERENCE CONCLUSIONS

The conference deliberations concentrated on the following major themes: (1) the legal significance of the Helsinki Final Act; (2) the question of domestic jurisdiction and nonintervention; (3) the scope and character of the human rights undertakings of the Helsinki Final Act; (4) the right to self-determination; and (5) follow-up and implementation.

*N.B.: This is not a formal conference report and consequently does not necessarily express the collective or individual opinions of the conference participants.

Legal Significance of the Helsinki Final Act

On this topic, the conference participants agreed that the Helsinki Final Act is a document of great moral and political importance, defining the common interests of the signatory states. It may eventually evolve into an historic milestone in European and Atlantic relations and come to be recognized as a symbol of ideological tolerance. (See Chapter 2.)

There was also general agreement that the Helsinki Final Act is not a treaty and that it does not in and of itself create legally binding obligations. It was strongly emphasized, however, that this conclusion should not detract from the great legal significance of the Helsinki Final Act. (See Chapters 2 through 5.) The following considerations, *inter alia,* were deemed by the conference participants to explain or relate to the legal significance of this instrument:

1. As an agreement among states, notwithstanding the fact that it is not legally binding, the Helsinki Final Act must be interpreted by reference to relevant principles of international law. That is, the international law concepts to which it refers, such as, for example, "domestic jurisdiction" and "intervention," must be understood to have their common international law meaning unless it clearly appears that the signatory states intended a different meaning.

2. Without being legally binding, the Helsinki Final Act establishes a valid basis, as between the signatory states, for seeking information and exchanging views on the Helsinki Final Act, for making demands for compliance with its provisions, and for monitoring such compliance. That is to say, although a signatory state's failure to comply with these demands does not give rise to a legal claim or legal remedies for nonperformance, the Act legitimates appropriate peaceful political action to obtain performance.

3. By incorporating and invoking preexisting principles of international law, the Helsinki Final Act confirms the adherence of the participating states to these principles and strengthens them to that extent. Moreover, various provisions of the Helsinki Final Act may be viewed as evidence of the practice of states relating to certain emerging rules of customary international law; they can assist in establishing authoritative interpretations of ambiguous

international instruments and pronouncements; and they could provide a basis for the development of new rules of international law. It is clear, in this connection, that the uses to which the Helsinki Final Act will be put by states in the years to come will determine its ultimate normative status and influence.

Domestic Jurisdiction and Nonintervention

The view which emerged from the conference deliberations on this question was: (1) that the conduct of a signatory state of the Helsinki Final Act relating to the human rights proclaimed in General Principle VII and Basket III was not a matter within the domestic jurisdiction of that state, and (2) that peaceful reaction to violations of any of these human rights provisions did not constitute intervention or any other unlawful or improper interference with the violating state. It was concluded, accordingly, that every signatory state is entitled to inform itself of the policies and actions of any other signatory state with regard to matters covered by the human rights provisions of the Helsinki Final Act; that any signatory state may negotiate with or make diplomatic representations to another signatory state about its compliance or noncompliance with these human rights clauses; that any such state may discuss compliance or noncompliance with these human rights undertakings by other signatory states in international organizations, at meetings of experts of the signatory states, or at any follow-up conference of their representatives of which the Belgrade meeting is the first. (See Chapter 3.)

There seemed to be agreement, too, that—whatever their desirability or effectiveness in particular circumstances—unilateral criticism or peaceful, noncoercive policies and acts in reaction to violations of human rights by other signatory states, even if designed to influence the violator to cease its violation, do not constitute intervention or other unlawful or improper interference with the signatory state.

Scope and Character of the Human Rights Undertakings of the Helsinki Final Act

On this subject, the conference participants concluded that no assessment of the human rights provisions of the Helsinki Final

Act should overlook the important differences in character between General Principle VII, on the one hand, and Basket III,
on the other.

General Principle VII was acknowledged to be a statement of
fundamental normative importance because it incorporates by
reference a vast body of existing conventional and customary international human rights law and contains the undertaking of the
signatory states to abide by this law. To the extent that the
provisions of General Principle VII are less restrictive or impose
more extensive obligations than do existing international human
rights undertakings, to that extent the signatories of the Helsinki
Final Act have (morally and politically) committed themselves to
conform to the standards set out in it. (See Chapter 5 for specific
examples; see also Chapter 4.)

The conference participants agreed, furthermore, that the express identification of certain human rights in some provisions of
General Principle VII (e.g., paragraphs 1, 3, and 4) indicates the
great importance that the signatory states attach to those rights
and to their enforcement and enjoyment. (See Chapter 7.) It was
also especially emphasized that, in General Principle VII, the
signatory states "confirm the right of the individual to know and
act upon his rights and duties" and that they undertake "to act in
conformity with the purposes and principles of the Charter of the
United Nations and with the Universal Declaration of Human
Rights." The reference, in this context, to the Universal
Declaration was deemed by the conference participants to be of
particular significance. Some of them expressed the view that certain signatory states had never before acknowledged so
unequivocally the normative status of the Universal Declaration.

The human rights provisions contained in Basket III, while no
less important in terms of the values and interests they are
designed to protect, are for the most part narrower in scope and
more specific in terms of the goals they attempt to achieve. The
provisions also establish important implementation priorities
which, it was agreed, should be monitored and adhered to. The
conference participants concluded, furthermore, that, whenever
the Basket III provisions are more specific than those set out in
various obligatory international human rights instruments on the
same subject, the former may be resorted to by the signatory
states to clarify the meaning of the latter, including the intended

reach of available defenses, limitations, and escape clauses found in some of these instruments. (See Chapters 4 and 5.)

The Right to Self-Determination

The conference participants reviewed and accepted the proposition that the right to self-determination proclaimed in General Principle VIII guarantees both external and internal self-determination of peoples on a universal basis. The right to self-determination enunciated in this provision was universal in the sense that it applied to all peoples and was not intended to be limited to peoples living under colonial or minority regimes. General Principle VIII could consequently be viewed either as providing added support for a comparable interpretation of the meaning of United Nations pronouncements on self-determination or as a significant evolution of that concept. (See Chapter 6.)

Follow-Up and Implementation

The conference participants shared the strong conviction that the human rights provisions of the Helsinki Final Act constituted the price the Western signatories had extracted from the East for important concessions made by the West, demonstrating the great value the West attached to these clauses. As a result, an unyielding insistence on compliance with these provisions was imperative to maintain the bargain. But it was also agreed that, initially, this objective could best be promoted by the signatory states through the exchange of information and views concerning the implementation of the human rights provisions and through suggestions for the improvement of the implementation processes. (For examples, see Chapter 7.)

The great importance the West attaches to human rights as an indispensable element of any lasting détente and a humane international order had to be made credible to the East. It was emphasized, however, that this result should and could be achieved without resorting to methods that threatened to destroy the confidence-building climate which the Helsinki Final Act was designed to nurture. The conference participants were accordingly convinced that Western demands that all signatory states comply with the human rights provisions of the Helsinki Final Act should be pursued in a spirit of cooperation, which avoided confrontation, recrimination, and self-righteous ideological sloganeering. The emphasis should be on measures, techniques, and processes capable of fulfilling the human rights promises of the Helsinki Final Act.*

---

*The conference participants discussed a number of specific follow-up proposals, but none of these could be reviewed in sufficient depth, nor was there enough time to develop priorities to rank and categorize them. It was consequently decided that they should not be reproduced as part of the "Conference Conclusions."

2 The Special Significance of the Helsinki Final Act

by SUZANNE BASTID

Any examination of the problem of human rights as it arises for the states participating in the Conference on Security and Cooperation in Europe presupposes that one has already drawn attention to the particular characteristics of the voluminous and unprecedented document—the Helsinki Final Act—which was solemnly adopted by the "High Representatives" of the participating states.

The uniqueness of this document must first be emphasized before the circumstances that explain it and the aims pursued by its draftsmen are discussed. It is only in this context that one can attempt to determine the scope of its human rights provisions.

I

The Final Act of the Helsinki conference is distinguished almost entirely by the way it contrasts with traditional diplomatic documents.

In the first place, the thirty-five participants do not represent a defined geographical whole, such as exists on the African or American continents. The participation of the United States and Canada indicates that the Final Act applies not only to relations between states in a given geographical zone but to the relations between states which have a direct interest in Europe. And this takes into consideration the presence on European soil of American and Canadian forces.

The existence of blocs has thus not been disregarded, but bloc-versus-bloc negotiation has been ruled out, because of the role played by the nonaligned states (among them, Finland, Switzerland and Yugoslavia) and because some states belonging to alliances (such as Romania) wished to ensure that they could express themselves individually without using an intermediary. The latter concept is expressed in a procedural rule adopted at the initiative of Romania, under which all the states participating in the conference do so as sovereign independent states and in conditions of full equality. The conference proceeded outside the framework of military alliances. The rotation of the conference chairmanship was intended to symbolize the principle of equality of rights.

Thus, although the selection of the participating states is determined both by geographical and by political considerations, the Final Act does not employ language comparable to that found in the treaties of Westphalia, which spoke of the King of Sweden, his allies and followers, nor does it make the distinction embodied in the treaty of Versailles, between major powers and other states.

Unlike treaties setting up organizations of a universal character, no provision is made in the Final Act for opening to other states the opportunity to join the established arrangement. Although the preamble to Basket I does mention the close link between peace and security in Europe and in the world as a whole, nothing is done to associate other states with the overall provisions of the Final Act. The conference did recognize, however, that the non-European states bordering the Mediterranean should be placed in a special category, but no specific procedure is laid down to maintain the contacts and dialogue referred to by the conference.

If one examines the content of the Final Act, its uniqueness is confirmed by the number of problems it deals with, the diversity of principles expounded by it, the multitude of rules it expresses, and the programs it formulates. It is striking that some of its provisions are related to principles contained in instruments of a universal scope and others are related to agreements of a limited scope. Certain original programs for action are also laid down. The scope of each provision must therefore be considered individually to determine whether it refers to an obligation established by another diplomatic instrument and whether implementation machinery already exists. This complexity is found in particular in relation to human rights. As a result, careful examination of each provision is necessary before conclusions can be arrived at.

Finally, the uniqueness of the Helsinki Final Act is illustrated by its legal scope: this point is of capital importance and is often overlooked. The term "Final Act of a diplomatic conference" in practice covers instruments that vary in effect according to the circumstances. The act contains, as is often the case, a brief summary of the conference, but the content of the test adopted by the "High Representatives of the participating States" does not constitute a multilateral treaty. This was formally pointed out during the third stage of the conference. The requirements for transmission to the Secretary General of the U.N. are not fulfilled, and the text of the Final Act itself is quite explicit in stating that it does not qualify for registration under Article 102 of the U.N. Charter. The tenth principle of the Declaration of Guiding Principles distinguishes clearly between legal obligations under international law and the application of the provisions set out at the conference.

It is thus clear that the participating states did not intend to bind themselves legally, and they expressly noted that the Declaration on Principles Guiding Relations between Participating States "does not affect their rights and obligations, nor the corresponding treaties and other agreements and arrangements."

Moreover, the document which emerged from the conference cannot be likened to the declarations of the U.N. General Assembly. The U.N. documents are adopted within the framework of an international organization and they emanate from a body which, while obviously also composed of state representatives, has a constitution that binds the member states and a defined competence subordinate to the rules of conventional origin relating to the conditions pursuant to which the will of the Organization is expressed. The Conference on Security and Cooperation in Europe convened under completely different conditions, in what one might call a classical diplomatic conference. It met and was organized on the basis of the sovereignty of the participating states, who agreed upon the negotiating procedure and who, in the exercise of their sovereignty, defined the consequences arising from the texts on which agreement was reached. Thus, even though the participating states, being members of universal organizations, made frequent references to their obligations in this regard and to the competences attributable to these organizations, the Final Act cannot legally be assimilated to a declaration adopted by the U.N. General Assembly. Each of its component parts must be considered to assess its exact scope. This preliminary and fundamental investigation, which is not an easy task, must be undertaken, particularly when addressing the problem of human rights. The titles of the various parts of the Final Act doubtless provide some initial guidance, but one must go further in the examination of this complex text to distinguish between what is an expression of the law in force and what appears to be a program of action whose terms are more or less defined, and which each state is called upon to implement on the domestic level or in its relations with third states.

Having deliberately ruled out the adoption of a treaty, the participating states wanted to bring to light, in the most solemn way, the importance which they attributed to the results of their work: the terms of the Final Act itself, and particularly its preamble, show the importance and the extent of the undertaking. The gathering of the heads of state and government at Helsinki for the signing ceremony, which recalls the great landmarks of world diplomacy, bears witness to this. But even more significant is the entirely novel provision pursuant to which "the text of this Final Act will be published in each participating State, which will disseminate it and make it known as widely as possible." Short of providing for its posting in every community, could any more original and significant provision have been inserted in the Final Act? Not only does it provide for publication different from that required by some constitutions for treaties—a publication which would not be required in this case—but the text speaks of "dissemination" and of making the Final Act "known as widely as possible." What else can this mean but that it is understood that the document is not intended exclusively for the authorities, but that the whole population should be able to know of it? This original provision has, of course, given rise to some controversy regarding the requirements for its implementation, but it is uncontested that the Final Act was published in full in *Pravda* and

Izvestia. In this way, the Final Act has become known to the population of the participating states.

II

The Final Act is an unusual document that defies all comparison. It deals with a very complicated political situation that is without precedent and requires a novel approach. The political situation in question contains three essential elements:

1. No treaty of peace was drawn up between Germany and her adversaries; the territorial rules that applied after the Second World War were therefore not regulated by traditional procedures.

2. Various agreements and arrangements dealing with German territory have gradually led to solutions of debatable effect, despite the admission of the Federal Republic of Germany and the German Democratic Republic to the United Nations.

3. Finally, and especially since the end of the Second World War, Europe has been the arena for the ideological confrontation that the phrases "iron curtain" and the "cold war" symbolize. The latter phrase covers a collection of practices comparable to international war and led to military alliances unaccompanied by any declared conflict.

The Helsinki Conference met at a time when it was felt necessary to confer formal international status on the territorial agreements that had previously been concluded. In particular, however, the conference was the expression of the political will "to broaden, deepen and make continuing and lasting the process of détente." It was not a question, as in other diplomatic conferences, of dividing territories or of granting particular advantages to one side or another, but of creating the conditions for a certain style of relations characterized largely by its contrast to what had gone before. Basically, it is a style of living which is at issue. The Final Act reflects an attempt to explore the many aspects of an effort that is directed towards the transformation of relations, while leaving to each state the "right freely to choose and develop its political, social, economic and cultural systems as well as its right to determine its laws and regulations." In addition, it recognizes the right "to be or not to be a party to bilateral or multilateral treaties including the right to be or not to be a party to treaties of alliance," as well as "the right of neutrality." The system of the Final Act accepts the political structure of Europe in all its diversity, but within this framework it seeks to improve and intensify the relations of European peoples. This effort is both audacious and without any direct precedent, which explains the unique character of the document itself. It is tempting, for that very reason, to compare the Final Act to the treaty of Osnabrück, which created the "détente" between Catholics and Protestants among the German states and, in particular, provided for the protection of the rights of individuals who were the subjects of Princes practicing another religious belief. After the armed struggle which preceded that treaty, it was time to base human relations on foundations of tolerance.

III

The specific experience acquired by the states participating in the conference gave them a common asset in the form of a procedure, a program and a framework.* This common asset should be preserved for the conduct of the talks at Belgrade.

In the first place, the procedure just referred to consisted in the organization of the Conference in three stages and at several levels. The provisions on the follow-up to the conference adopted were: the system of a preparatory meeting, followed by a meeting of the representatives designated by the Ministers for Foreign Affairs, the option of further similar meetings and the possibility of a second conference. The Final Act provides, moreover, that the procedural provisions of the conference will be applied to these meetings. This confirms the principle that decisions will be taken by consensus, as well as the principle of the equality of the participating states as far as concerns their representation on the working bodies and their right to express their own positions.

In addition, there is the "program for better relations between the participating States" which relates to a variety of fields. Even the most superficial reading of the Final Act reveals a preoccupation, after the fundamental principles applicable to states as

*Andreani, *La Conférence sur la sécurité et la cooperation en Europe,* COLLOQUE DE BORDEAUX, Société francaise pour le droit international 113 (1977).

political entities have been enumerated, with the selection of fields in which obstacles have been encountered. Some objectives are formulated, accompanied by concrete proposals providing practical guidance for their implementation, whether through cooperation between states or through the facilitation or authorization of cooperation between individuals and groups with their counterparts in other states. It has rightly been pointed out that this is not a precise program accompanied by a statement of the measures to be taken, or by time limits. But the combination of objectives and measures of implementation, as outlined in the Final Act, should in time permit an assessment of the extent to which the elements of this program have been acted upon, opening the way to go beyond "the abstract conceptions of détente."

Finally, the conference not only established institutions, but also a means of assuring continuity. It specifically resolved "to continue the multilateral process initiated by the Conference." The necessary provisions to convene a further conference, the date and the place, are specified. But in doing so, the Final Act also introduces the principle of rotation between states and stipulates that the host country provide the technical secretariat of the follow-up meeting. This arrangement rules out the risk that the secretariat will be used to create the beginnings of an international organization.

Although the participating states recognize that the conference itself has enabled them to achieve some progress in improving security and developing co-operation in Europe, the Final Act indicates an understanding that this process must be continued. The aim of the Belgrade meeting is twofold. On the one hand, it is to proceed to "a thorough exchange of views both on the implementation of the provisions of the Final Act and of the tasks defined by the Conference;" and, on the other hand, it is to engage in an exchange of views on "the development of the process of détente in the future."

This wording merits some attention. It does not create the type of review procedure that is provided for in numerous treaties, operating either through reports submitted by the states parties or through complaints concerning their conduct. Instead, it is reminiscent of the system of commissions entrusted with the examination of the conditions of implementation of a treaty or even with proposing certain amendments thereto. Such a machinery has at times taken on very original forms when linked to a treaty establishing a far-reaching program giving expression to a new political will, as is illustrated by the Franco-German treaty of 1963. But in the case of the Final Act of Helsinki, the magnitude of the effort and the nature of the task defined therein gives the "thorough exchange of views" a completely original character. That it is permissible, to achieve the above-mentioned ends, to raise the various questions dealt with in the Final Act is hardly in doubt; that views can be stated on initiatives connected with the objectives or measures of implementation provided for in the act is also certain; that information can be obtained on the interpretation of a particular provision or on the time taken to act upon what was decided in the agreement and that opinions can be given on a divergence of views as to what is required by the process of détente is no doubt also permissible. But it can hardly be denied that such initiatives do not appear to be consistent with the system and fundamental aim of détente, unless the measures of application have been defined in fairly concrete terms, as is the case, for example, with regard to "human contacts" and information.

Principle VII of the Declaration on Principles Guiding Relations between Participating States, which the states declared it to be "their determination to respect and put into practice," refers to respect for human rights and fundamental freedoms, including the freedom of thought, conscience, religion or belief. In addition, the declaration reaffirms the principle of nonintervention in internal affairs (Principle VII) and the right of each state "to determine its laws and regulations" (Principle I). It should be added that reference is made in the declaration to various human rights instruments which are of interest to the participating states or to which they are parties. To what extent and under what conditions the thorough exchange of views at Belgrade might relate to Principle VII of the declaration is a difficult question, and one that no doubt raises quite different problems with regard to Basket III.

Basket III, "Cooperation in Humanitarian and Other Fields," is placed in the context of the principles governing the relations between participating states set out in the declaration. But unlike Principle VII of the declaration, Basket III lists certain objectives: human contacts, information, cooperation and exchanges in the field of culture, and cooperation and exchanges in the field of education. It also enumerates the measures of implementation, which consist either of procedures or contacts or cooperation with a view to reducing the obstacles to exchanges and movement. Sometimes unilateral action of the state is called for and sometimes concerted action between states or participation in international organizations is required.

In this field, the provisions of the Helsinki Final Act have tried ingeniously to address certain difficulties that had in fact given rise to the cold war. It is without doubt in this context, subject to the reservations indicated above, that the exchange of views of Belgrade could principally take place, provided there is a desire to continue working within the system and to proceed periodically to adjustments which experience might show to be necessary.

3 Human Rights and "Domestic Jurisdiction"

by LOUIS HENKIN

Charges that various parties to the Helsinki Final Act have not been complying with its human rights provisions have, of course, evoked denials as well as counter-charges against other participants. Some accused governments have also insisted, however, that, regardless of Helsinki, how they treat their own inhabitants is a matter within their domestic jurisdiction, and that scrutiny and censure by other governments constitute intervention and are unlawful.

"Domestic jurisdiction" and its counterpart "nonintervention" have confused and bedeviled international human rights activities since their inception. Volumes of official debate and scholarly comment have been devoted to these terms, particularly as regards the human rights activities of the United Nations, in the light of Article 2(7) of the U.N. Charter.[1] Before and since Helsinki, even statements by high government officials have reflected fundamental misunderstanding of the concepts, their import, and their limitations.

Much of the confusion about these terms derives from the tendency in international diplomatic life to confound legal concepts with political rhetoric, particularly as regards concepts that speak to the essential tension between national autonomy and international accountability. Confusion results, too, from the fact that, while domestic jurisdiction and nonintervention are legal terms used in legal documents, there is hardly agreement on the boundaries between domestic and international jurisdiction, or on what constitutes intervention or other impermissible interference.

For all their heavy freight of rhetoric and their penumbra of uncertainty, as legal terms both domestic jurisdiction and nonintervention have hard cores of agreed meaning. Domestic jurisdiction is that which is not a proper subject of foreign or international concern; what is not, in plain words, anyone else's business.[2] *That which is governed by international law or agreement is ipso facto and by definition not a matter of domestic jurisdiction.*[3] Short of direct legal obligation, moreover, many domestic matters are only defeasibly domestic, and may become legitimate subjects of international attention because a state had submitted to international or foreign jurisdiction by some general undertaking, for example, the U.N. Charter establishing the jurisdiction of U.N. organs.

"Intervention" is an effort to bring influence to bear on other governments by particular means. Although there are occasional references to unlawful intervention and some circumstances where intervention is said to be justified, strictly intervention is better defined as unlawful interference; and what by definition constitutes intervention is *ipso facto* unlawful. Treaties and declarations, and the Final Act at Helsinki itself, forbid intervention (not merely unlawful intervention).

International law forbids intervention in matters that are within the domestic jurisdiction of another state. If a matter is not within the domestic jurisdiction of another state, external or international concern with it cannot be intervention. Beyond any dispute or doubt, *it is not intervention or other improper interference for one state to respond to violations by another of her obligations under international law or agreement* [though some forms of external or international reaction may be barred by other legal doctrine, e.g., the unilateral use of force under Article 2(4) of the U.N. Charter]. It is not intervention for an international body to consider a matter within its granted jurisdiction.[4]

Strictly, moreover, intervention means dictatorial interference by force or threat of force. Lesser forms of interference may be bad (diplomatic) manners, and some may roil friendly relations but generally do not violate any principle of universal international law. It is not intervention, or other interference forbidden by law, for a government to express views about, or even to criticize publicly, the actions of other governments which are distasteful to it, for example, the political ideology guiding other governments or their economic and social systems. Surely, in the absence of agreement to the contrary, it is not intervention or other improper interference for one state to shape its own policies (say, on trade) and the warmth of its relations on the basis of taste or distaste for actions of other governments, even as regards matters that are strictly their own affair and even if done to influence the other governments' behavior in these matters.

As blanket objections to international concern with human rights, the claims of domestic jurisdiction and nonintervention have been long dead.[5] Surely, there are some circumstances in which the condition of human rights is a legitimate concern of and a basis for appropriate action by other states or international organizations. Surely, there are some responses that international organizations or individual states can make to infringements of human rights that are not interventions or other unlawful interferences in the affairs of the violating state. If human rights were always a matter of domestic jurisdiction and never a proper subject of external attention in any form, provisions of the U.N. Charter, the Universal Declaration of Human Rights, the various international covenants and conventions, and countless activities, resolutions, and actions of the U.N. and other international bodies would be *ultra vires*; every government would be guilty of meddling and some also of intervention; and numerous nongovernmental organizations and millions of individuals would have labored egregiously and in vain for decades. Helsinki itself assumed that human rights are a proper subject of international attention. Human rights were on the international agenda for consideration at the highest levels of government; human rights undertakings were exchanged among many governments for undertakings about international security and trade, and the Final Act included respect for human rights as one of the Principles Guiding Relations between Participating States. Any suggestions that the human rights Basket of Helsinki is not of legitimate concern to other parties would vitiate all the other understandings and undertakings that depended on it and would nullify the entire accords.

The domestic jurisdiction objection to external attention to human rights is worthy of any legal (or political) notice only if asserted narrowly and precisely. One might consider the following arguments.

1. How a state treats its own nationals is not a matter of international concern unless the state has assumed international legal obligations governing such treatment. There is no customary international law of human rights and no international agreement to which all states are party. While almost all states have adhered to the U.N. Charter, they did not thereby assume any binding normative obligation to respect the human rights of their own citizens. The Universal Declaration of Human Rights, too, did not create any legal obligation for any state. The Final Act at Helsinki, not being legally binding, created no human rights obligations for the participants.

2. While states party to an international agreement (e.g. the International Covenant on Civil and Political Rights or the Convention on the Elimination of All Forms of Racial Discrimination) undertake to comply with its provisions, they do not thereby submit to any scrutiny or censure nor to any procedures, remedies, or claims for violations other than those expressly provided for in the agreement. In particular, unless agreed otherwise, such agreements do not create legal obligations by one party towards another and do not give one party any legal interest in compliance by other parties or any right to enforce the agreement and invoke legal remedies against other parties.

3. The Helsinki Accord cannot be the basis for any response or remedy by another state because they do not constitute legal obligations. In any event, the Final Act does not authorize claims, complaints, criticisms, or any other recourse by one participating state against another for alleged violations of human rights generally or of any particular provision in the Final Act. The part of the Final Act titled "Follow Up to the Conference" provides only for negotiation and exchange of views and for further meetings. And the Final Act declares that "the participating States will refrain from any intervention, direct or indirect, individual or collective, in the internal or external affairs falling within the domestic jurisdiction of another participating State, regardless of their mutual relations."

4. Except as otherwise expressly provided in some international agreement, a criticism or protest by one state that another is violating human rights, even that it is violating international obligations to respect human rights, constitutes intervention or is otherwise impermissible. It is impermissible for

one government to deal directly with, support, or encourage nationals of another state in their attempt to seek redress, even if they allege that they are victims of human rights violations. It is impermissible for one state to attempt to coerce another to modify its domestic policies on human rights, e.g., by manipulating trade arrangements or offers of aid or by criticism and unfriendly statements.

These arguments are generally misconceived and ill-founded. My thesis may be briefly stated:

1. Virtually all states are now subject to some international law and obligation as regards at least some human rights of their inhabitants. To that extent their actions in regard to such human rights are, of course, not within their domestic jurisdiction; and external scrutiny and efforts to bring about compliance with the human rights obligations are not intervention or other improper interference in domestic affairs.

2. Unless the agreement provides otherwise, any party to an international agreement on human rights has, against another party who has violated the agreement, the remedies and recourses available generally for breach of an international agreement. Unless the agreement provides otherwise, any special machinery provided for implementing its human rights obligations does not replace but merely supplements the usual remedies for breach of international agreement.

3. That the Helsinki Accord is not legally binding means there are no legal remedies for their violation; adherence to the Accord is nonetheless an international undertaking and violation of them is a proper basis for international (nonlegal) recourse and remedy by other participants. Insistence by other adherents that the accords be honored and the peaceful means that they might use to induce compliance with these international undertakings are not interventions or other impermissible interferences in domestic affairs, but rather, the proper and normal means and methods of the international system.

4. Intervention forbidden by international law signifies dictatorial interference. A state's expression of criticism or distaste or its policies modifying relations of trade, aid, or other intercourse with governments because they violate human rights are not interventions but legitimate acts of self-interest that are a state's own affair and within its own domestic jurisdiction.

INTERNATIONAL HUMAN RIGHTS OBLIGATIONS

There are now numerous international agreements dealing in whole or in part with human rights. Matters covered by these human rights undertakings are, of course, not within the domestic jurisdiction of the states party to them.

The Human Rights Obligations of U.N. Members

Almost all states are parties to the U.N. Charter and bound by its human rights provisions. By adhering to the U.N. Charter, states expressly "pledge themselves to take joint and separate action in cooperation with" the U.N. organization to promote "universal respect for, and observance of, human rights and fundamental freedoms for all without distinction as to race, sex, language, or religion" (Articles 55, 56).

That states "pledge themselves" imports legal obligation; but there has not been agreement among governments, or among commentators, as to the import and content of that obligation. While some governments and commentators have considered it only a general requirement of cooperation that has no normative content, others have urged that important infringements of generally-agreed human rights are violations of Articles 55 and 56. Some have argued that, while the undertakings in the U.N. Charter were inchoate and general, they were realized and particularized in the Universal Declaration of Human Rights; so that all parties to the U.N. Charter are legally obligated to abide by the provisions in the Universal Declaration. Yet another view has it that the U.N. Charter, the Universal Declaration, the various international conventions, resolutions of U.N. organs and other multilateral bodies, and the practices of states have combined to create customary, or a blend of customary and conventional, legal obligations upon all states to respect at least some human rights norms.

There has been no resolution of these diverse views and no authoritative definition of the human rights obligations of states under the U.N. Charter and under legal developments since the U.N. Charter. United Nations practice since 1945, including numerous resolutions, one or more of which was supported by almost every state, clearly reflects a prevailing view that the

U.N. Charter has at least some normative import and content.[6] Repeated resolutions have declared that apartheid in South Africa is contrary to the U.N. Charter.[7] In its advisory opinion on Namibia, the International Court of Justice declared the extension and continuation of apartheid in Namibia to be "a flagrant violation of the purposes and principles of the Charter."[8] In 1967, by an overwhelming vote, the Economic and Social Council (ECOSOC) extended the interpretation of the U.N. Charter to reach beyond racial discrimination, authorizing the Commission on Human Rights to study "situations which reveal a consistent pattern of violations of human rights, as exemplified by the policy of apartheid. . ."[9] In 1970 ECOSOC approved a procedure for considering private communications "which appear to reveal a consistent pattern of gross and reliably attested violations of human rights and fundamental freedoms. . . ."[10] Even states (e.g., the USSR) which had opposed this procedure and the interpretation of the U.N. Charter it implied later joined in action by the Commission on Human Rights, approved by the General Assembly, to investigate alleged violations of human rights in Chile.[11] In its opinion in the *Barcelona Traction Case* , the International Court of Justice said that there are universal obligations deriving "for example, in contemporary international law, from the outlawing of acts of aggression, and of genocide, as also from the principles and rules concerning the basic rights of the human person, including protection from slavery and racial discrimination."[12] In 1976, in the commentary to its draft articles on state responsibility, the International Law Commission concluded that "international law now in force" includes obligations of "essential importance for safe-guarding the human being, such as those prohibiting slavery, genocide and apartheid."[13]

It is difficult to avoid the conclusion that some violations of human rights (e.g., apartheid and other forms of racial discrimination, genocide, slavery, or torture), in addition to being violations of particular conventions if committed by parties to such conventions, are violations of the U.N. Charter for any U.N. member, if not of customary international law binding on all states. The generality of states have supported the view that "a consistent pattern of gross violations of human rights" is now a violation of international law and obligation if practiced by any party to the U.N. Charter and even perhaps, by nonmembers.[14]

Such violations surely are not a matter of domestic jurisdiction. Whether an alleged infringement is such a violation is a question of international law, not one for an accused state to determine finally.

Parties to Particular Conventions

Some parties to the Helsinki Final Act have adhered also to particular international agreements on human rights, e.g., the Convention on the Prevention and Punishment of the Crime of Genocide, the International Convention on the Elimination of All Forms of Racial Discrimination, the International Covenant on Civil and Political Rights and its Protocol, and the International Covenant on Economic, Social, and Cultural Rights. No state party can invoke domestic jurisdiction as regards matters covered by any convention.

Human Rights Undertakings at Helsinki

At the Conference on Security and Cooperation in Europe the participating states agreed to discuss human rights together with other matters relating to security and cooperation. In the Final Act, the participants declared it to be among the principles guiding relations between them that they would respect human rights and fundamental freedoms and promote and encourage their effective exercise. In addition:

> In the field of human rights and fundamental freedoms, the participating States will act in conformity with the purposes and principles of the Charter of the United Nations and with the Universal Declaration of Human Rights. They will also fulfil their obligations as set forth in the international declarations and agreements in this field, including inter alia the International Covenants on Human Rights, by which they may be bound. (1(a)VII)

They also agreed to fulfil in good faith obligations under international law generally (1(a)X). Later in the act (Basket III) the participating states "make it their aim," "declare their readiness," and "express their intention" to implement cooperation in humanitarian and other fields, including human contacts, information, and cooperation and exchange in culture and in education. These human rights provisions were the condition and the price of other provisions of great political importance desired by other participants. Western participants saw them as the condition of and an integral aspect of détente at which the whole Final Act aimed.

While Helsinki was not intended to be a legally binding agreement, and does not add legally binding human rights obligations, it clearly precludes any suggestion that matters it deals with are within domestic jurisdiction and beyond the reach of appropriate inquiry and recourse. Gentlemen's agreements and other nonbinding political and moral undertakings are established instruments in international relations, and their violation brings important political and moral consequences. Speaking of nonbinding international agreements, Professor Oscar Schachter said recently:

> The fact that the states have entered into mutual engagements confers an entitlement on each party to make representations to the other on the execution of those engagements. It becomes immaterial whether the conduct in question was previously regarded as entirely discretionary or within the reserved domain of domestic jurisdiction. By entering into an international pact with other states, a party may be presumed to have agreed that the matters covered are no longer exclusively within its concerns.[15]

RESPONSE TO VIOLATION OF HUMAN RIGHTS OBLIGATIONS

Breach of a human rights obligation, like violation of any international legal obligation, is an international wrongful act for which the international legal system provides remedies. It has been suggested, however, that the only remedies for the violation of a human rights agreement are those specified in the agreement. In particular, unless expressly so provided, one party does not have a remedy against another for failure to live up to the agreement. That view is ill-founded.

The duty to carry out international obligations is the heart of the international legal system; and that prime duty implies an ancillary duty to cease and desist from a violation and to give other satisfaction to the state or states to which the obligation was due. The injured state may seek reparation and ask that the violator take measures to prevent repetition, offer an apology, punish the persons who committed the violation, pay a symbolic sum of money, or afford other relief.[16]

Except for the few universal obligations, enforceable perhaps by any state (in a kind of *actio popularis*),[17] a breach of an international obligation is a wrong to the particular state or states to which that obligation is due, and only such state or states may enforce that obligation and seek a remedy for its violation. An international agreement creates obligations between parties and gives each party a legal interest in having it carried out; it may be enforced by one party against another even if it is an agreement for the benefit of a third entity not party to the agreement. Of course, parties may modify these general principles in particular cases. Thus, expressly or by clear implication from the nature of the agreement or from some of its provisions, a multilateral agreement may contemplate enforcement of the agreement only by a party directly aggrieved, not by all parties. (Some multilateral treaties are essentially a series of bilateral arrangements, so that a violation affecting only a particular other party is to be enforced only by that party.) A multilateral agreement will frequently establish special remedies for violation, and may expressly or by implication provide that these shall replace (rather than supplement) traditional interstate remedies.

The argument that human rights agreements are not directly enforceable between the parties is not based on any notion that the subject matter is in the domestic jurisdiction of the parties. It does not deny that human rights agreements create legal obligations or that the law provides remedies for violation of these obligations as for others. The argument seems to be based, rather, on the view that, as a matter of interpretation, human rights agreements in general, and particular human rights agreements, contemplate no remedies between parties, but only whatever remedies are expressly provided. It is assumed that states are willing to enter into agreements about human rights but are unwilling to have them enforced among the parties; the quest for special enforcement machinery, it is said, also reflects the intention that ordinary interstate remedies be excluded.

These arguments are not persuasive. International human rights agreements are like other international agreements, creating legal obligations between the parties and international responsibility for their violation. They are essentially mutual undertakings among states for the benefit of third parties (the inhabitants of the countries party to the agreement) and in principle are enforceable by the promisees, that is, the other parties to the agreement. *Prima facie,* surely, and in the absence of any expressed or clearly implied intention to supersede them, the usual remedies for breach of an international obligation are available here.

Because violation by a state of the rights of its own inhabitants does not directly injure other states party to the agreement, it was recognized that other parties may be reluctant to seem officious and incur the political onus of calling a violator to account. It was thought, too, that such protection by another party might often not be an effective remedy for violations. Hence, the continuing efforts to develop special machinery to implement human rights obligations. But there is nothing in the character of human rights obligations, or in the principal human rights agreements, that suggests that such machinery is exclusive and is intended to replace the ordinary remedies available to any party to an agreement for breach by another party. The draftsmen of multilateral agreements recognized that other parties may be reluctant to enforce the agreement; there is no evidence that they intended to deny parties the legal right to do so and to eliminate the ordinary legal consequences of international undertakings and the ordinary remedies for their violation.

The effort to create an international law of human rights has been largely a struggle to develop effective machinery to implement agreed norms. Arduous effort has not brought forth machinery of notable effectiveness. It would be ironic if the meager successes in establishing such machinery should become the basis for interpreting the agreements as excluding other traditional means of enforcement, where they are most needed, and for denying them to states willing to use them. That the true beneficiaries of these agreements, the individuals inhabiting the territories of the parties, are usually not afforded an effective remedy (or any remedy at all) argues rather against finding that the other parties, the promisees, have no remedy either.

No human rights agreements, even those that establish elaborate enforcement machinery, expressly or by clear implication exclude the ordinary interstate remedies. In fact, the principal human rights agreements clearly imply the contrary: that every party to the agreement has a legal interest in having it observed by other parties and can invoke ordinary legal remedies to enforce it.[18] The first postwar, universal human rights agreement, the Genocide Convention, provides:

> Disputes between the Contracting Parties relating to the interpretation, application or fulfilment of the present Convention, including those relating to the responsibility of a State for genocide or for any of the other acts enumerated in Article III, shall be submitted to the International Court of Justice at the request of any of the parties to the dispute. (Article IX)

Providing jurisdiction for the International Court of Justice clearly recognized that every party retained legal interest in having other parties live up to their obligations under the Genocide Convention and might wish to resort to the usual legal remedies to vindicate that interest.

In more recent human rights agreements, especial concern for human rights and the desire to provide additional incentives for states to comply with human rights obligations led to the establishment of special enforcement machinery, for example, the special committees to see to the implementation of the International Convention on the Elimination of All Forms of Racial Discrimination and the International Covenant on Civil and Political Rights, or the more elaborate enforcement system under the European Convention on Human Rights. Such special enforcement arrangements, however, were clearly intended to supplement not to supplant general remedies available to one party against violation by another. The International Covenant on Civil and Political Rights, for example, makes this plain:

> The provisions for the implementation of the present Covenant. . . shall not prevent the States Parties to the present Covenant from having recourse to other procedures for settling a dispute in accordance with general or special international agreements in force between them. (Article 44)[19]

Again, the preservation of other procedures for settling disputes can only imply that the parties had legal interests in the enforcement of the agreement, interests which they might seek to vindicate by such alternative procedures.[20]

In other agreements, too, the normal rights and remedies of parties to human rights agreements are implied. Having established elaborate enforcement machinery, the European Convention provided:

> The High Contracting Parties agree that, except by special agreement, they will not avail themselves of treaties, conventions or declarations in force between them for the purpose of submitting, by way of

petition, a dispute arising out of the interpretation or application of this Convention to a means of settlement other than those provided for in this Convention. (Article 62)

There is no suggestion here, I note, that the human rights of all individuals everywhere can be protected by all states. Human rights agreements generally do not create universal legal interests for all states: they create legal interests for the parties to the agreement by virtue of the legal obligations assumed by them *inter sese.*[21] The remedies to be invoked are not by way of some ex-individuals everywhere can be protected by all states. Human rights agreements generally do not create universal legal interests for all states: they create legal interests for the parties to the agreement by virtue of the legal obligations assumed by them *inter sese.*[21] The remedies to be involved are not by way of some ex-traordinary *actio popularis;* they are the ordinary remedies available to parties to an agreement against violation by another party. The distinction is fundamental and clear. In the *South West Africa Cases,* for example, the majority denied the standing of Ethiopia and Liberia to enforce the human rights provisions of the mandate because they "were not parties to them. . . Not being parties to the instruments of mandate, they could draw from them only such rights as are unequivocally conferred."[22] The implication is that, even for the majority of the court, had the petitioners been parties to the mandate agreement they would have had a legal interest to enforce it and could have availed themselves of the usual remedies for vindicating that interest.

The suggestion that human rights agreements are generally not enforceable by the parties apparently reflects a fear that parties may resort to reprisal and other forcible remedies. But in general, the unilateral use of force in response to human rights violations is forbidden by the U.N. Charter. The danger that diplomatic protection, hitherto available only to a state's nationals against foreign governments, would now be provided by all governments party to a convention to all the inhabitants of any other party state, is also greatly exaggerated. States will not lightly risk their relations with another on behalf of the human rights of the latter's inhabitants. No doubt such responses would be used with prudence and infrequently, at most when there is "a serious breach on a widespread scale" of important provisions or a "consistent pattern of gross violations."[23] But as a matter of law, such protection is available, the consequence of a breach of international human rights obligations.[24]

Responses by Participants at Helsinki

Most of the participants at Helsinki are parties to the U.N. Charter and bound by its human rights provisions. Some of the participants are also parties to particular conventions, e.g., on genocide, racial discrimination, civil and political rights. These participants are entitled to monitor and take legal recourse against violations of those agreements by other participants party to them.

At Helsinki the participants made compliance with their undertakings to respect human rights and to carry out human rights undertakings made elsewhere in legally-binding international agreements the proper concern of all other Helsinki parties. Respect for human rights was one of the principles as to which the participants:

> Declare their determination to respect and put into practice each of them in its relations with all other participating States, irrespective of their political, economic or social systems as well as of their size, geographical location or level of economic development, the following principles, which all are of primary significance, guiding their mutual relations. . . . The participating States recognize the universal significance of human rights and fundamental freedoms, respect for which is an essential factor for the peace, justice and well-being necessary to ensure the development of friendly relations and cooperation among themselves as among all States.

The participants also declared their resolve, in the period following the conference, to pay due regard to and implement the provisions of the Final Act, unilaterally, bilaterally, and multilaterally; and to continue the multilateral process by a thorough exchange of views on implementation of the Final Act and by multilateral meetings to that end, the first of which was held in Belgrade in 1977.

Respect *vel non* for human rights, then, is a proper subject for discussion "bilaterally, by negotiation with other participating states"; "multilaterally, by meetings of experts of the participating states, and also within the framework of existing international organizations. . ."; and for a "thorough exchange of views on [their] implementation" at meetings like the one at Belgrade. Surely, there is no obstacle, indeed there would seem to be an affirmative political and moral commitment, for all participants to monitor the behavior of all other participants on human rights matters covered by the Final Act and to engage in bilateral and multilateral discussions about the implementation of the political and moral undertakings in the Final Act and of any antecedent legal undertakings that the Final Act incorporates by reference. What is provided as follow-up would seem to include the ordinary remedies available to one party for breach of political and moral undertakings by another; surely, there is nothing in the Final Act (or in international law) that precludes such peaceful bilateral responses.

NONINTERVENTION

The confusions and uncertainties of nonintervention are also largely irrelevant here. Whether in its traditional unwritten conception, in the principles of the U.N. Declaration on Friendly Relations, or in the principles adopted at Helsinki (which derive from the Declaration on Friendly Relations), the obligation not to intervene applies only to matters within a state's domestic jurisdiction. By virtue of the U.N. Charter and its aftermath, of particular conventions, or of Helsinki itself, human rights are not a matter of domestic jurisdiction and concern with them cannot be intervention or other impermissible interference.[25]

Surely it is not intervention, or any other improper interference, for a state party to an international agreement to have legal recourse or to react in other accepted lawful ways to violations of the agreement by others. Any member of the U.N., therefore, may properly respond to violations of charter norms, at least to a "consistent pattern of gross violations" of human rights.[26] Any party to a particular convention, in addition to invoking special remedies provided by the agreement, may have legal recourse or respond in other accepted lawful ways to any violation of any provision in the agreement. Any participant at Helsinki may monitor the behavior of all other participants in regard to any undertaking in the Final Act and may have appropriate political recourse in response to violations of those political commitments. In addition, Helsinki provides for other bilateral and multilateral follow-up.

None of these responses and remedies is in any way precluded by the guiding principle on Non-Intervention in Internal Affairs included in the Final Act:

> The participating States will refrain from any intervention, direct or indirect, individual or collective, in the internal or external affairs falling within the domestic jurisdiction of another participating State, regardless of their mutual relations. [1(a)VI]

To the extent covered by the U.N. Charter, by particular conventions, or the Helsinki Accords, human rights are not "within the domestic jurisdiction of another participating State."[27] All the other clauses in that principle also apply only as regards matters within a state's domestic jurisdiction, not, therefore, to its human rights undertakings.[28] Efforts by one participant to induce compliance by another with the human rights undertakings of the Final Act cannot be an act of "coercion designed to subordinate to their own interest the exercise by another participating State of the rights inherent in its sovereignty. . . ."

The principle of nonintervention is also irrelevant to common forms of external concern with human rights for other reasons. As a legal concept, intervention signifies "dictatorial interference." It "must either be forcible or backed by threat of force."[29] Scrutiny, criticism, or even encouragement or support to victims of human rights violations is not intervention (and would not be intervention even if human rights had remained a matter of domestic jurisdiction) even if it is designed to modify the target government's behavior in regard to human rights.

Neither, it should be clear, is it intervention or other impermissible interference for one state to shape its own policies in ways that will influence the behavior of other governments on human rights. Every state is free to shape its policies to bring about corresponding change in the behavior of others. Such influence, no matter how effective, is implicit in voluntary relations between nations, and is the foundation of all agreements between them whether tacit or expressed. In the absence of international agreement to the contrary, a state's policies in regard to foreign trade or aid or other forms of international intercourse and relationship are her own affair, a matter of her own domestic jurisdiction. No state is legally required to be more friendly than it wishes to be with another state which violates human rights.

At Helsinki, the West paid in valuable political coin for political and moral undertakings in regard to human rights. In effect, the Final Act confirms that respect for human rights by all is indispensable to détente and is an integral aspect of détente, as are security, refraining from the use of force, territorial integrity, and inviolability of frontiers. Each party agreed to "respect each other's right freely to choose and develop its political, social, economic, and cultural systems as well as its rights to determine its law and regulations"; but made it clear that requesting compliance with human rights obligations was not an intrusion upon sovereignty. They agreed not to intervene in matters falling within each other's domestic jurisdiction, but made it clear that human rights were not a matter of domestic jurisdiction and that calling a state to account for violating human rights was not intervention. In fact, they agreed to build into détente mutual monitoring, negotiation, peaceful exertions of influence, pursuit of legal remedies, and requests for satisfaction in regard to each participant's observance of human rights, as much as to its respect for the interests of others in security or trade.

NOTES

1. "Nothing contained in the present Charter shall authorize the United Nations to intervene in matters which are essentially within the domestic jurisdiction of any state or shall require the Members to submit such matters to settlement under the present Charter; but this principle shall not prejudice the application of enforcement measures under Chapter VII."

2. Political as well as legal writing have often treated domestic jurisdiction and international concern as mutually exclusive. While domestic jurisdiction has become a legal concept (as in Article 2(7) of the U.N. Charter), international concern is less clearly so except when used as meaning strictly "not a matter of domestic jurisdiction." While the phrase is here used in that sense, for convenience it is sometimes used colloquially also, but without having legal significance attributed to it.

3. Where the line lies between domestic and international jurisdiction is itself a question of international law, not one which any party can decide finally for itself. See the advisory opinion of the Permanent Court of International Justice in Tunis-Morocco Nationality Decrees Case, P.C.I.J. Ser. B., No. 4, 1 Hudson, World Ct. Rep. 143; Rights of Passage over Indian Territory Case, [1960] I.C.J. Rep. 33; Interpretation of Peace Treaties Case, [1950] I.C.J. 70-71; Compare Publications of the European Court of Human Rights, Belgian Linguistic Case (preliminary objections) judgment of February 9, 1967, Series A. at 16-20. In rare circumstances a state may reserve to itself the right to determine whether a matter is within its domestic jurisdiction. See, e.g., the U.S. Declaration recognizing as compulsory the jurisdiction of the International Court of Justice, [1975-76] I.C.J.Y.B. 80.

4. In general, U.N. practice reflects the view that international discussion, perhaps even declarations, recommendations, and judgments of the General Assembly, are not in-

terventions by the U.N. forbidden by Article 2(7). In practice, too, U.N. bodies have asserted authority to determine whether a U.N. action would be intervention contrary to that article. See R. HIGGINS, THE DEVELOPMENT OF INTERNATIONAL LAW THROUGH THE POLITICAL ORGANS OF THE UNITED NATIONS 4 (1963). But *cf.* Watson, *Autointerpretation, Competence, and the Continuing Validity of Article* 2(7) *of the U.N. Charter* 71 AM. J. INT'L L. 60 (1977).

5. See, generally, Ermacora, *Human Rights and Domestic Jurisdiction,* 2 RECUEIL DES COURS 371 (1968).

6. While much U.N. practice may be justified in part on the view that U.N. consideration does not constitute intervention within the meaning of Article 2(7), there are innumerable indications that many members of the U.N. considered some alleged infringements of human rights to be violations of the U.N. Charter. See L. Sohn and T. Buergenthal, INTERNATIONAL PROTECTION OF HUMAN RIGHTS 505-997 (1973).

7. *See, e.g.,* the first of many resolutions, Res. 721 (VIII), 8 December 1953, 8 GAOR, Supp. No. 17 (a/2630) at 67 (1953). *See* the materials collected in Sohn and Buergenthal above, note 6, at 634-739.

8. The advisory opinion on the legal consequences for states of the continued presence of South Africa in Namibia, [1971] I.C.J. 16, para. 131, stated:

Under the Charter of the United Nations, the former Mandatory had pledged itself to observe and respect, in a territory having an international status, human rights and fundamental freedoms for all without distinction as to race. To establish instead, and to enforce, distinctions, exclusions, restrictions and limitations exclusively based on grounds of race, colour, descent or national or ethnic origin which constitute a denial of fundamental human rights is a flagrant violation of the purposes and principles of the Charter.

See Schwelb, *The International Court of Justice and the Human Rights Clauses of the Charter,* 66 AM. J. INT'L L. 337 (1972).

9. ECOSOC Res. 1235 (XLII) 6 June 1967, 42 ESCOR, Supp. No. 1 (E/4393) at 17-18. See also ECOSOC Res. 1102 (XL), 4 March 1966, 40 ESCOR, Supp. No. 1 (2/4176) at 6.

10. ECOSOC Res. 1503 (XLVIII), 27 May 1970, 48 ESCOR, Supp. No. 1 A (E/4832/Add.1) at 8-9.

11. In 1974, the Commission on Human Rights sent a telegram to the government of Chile protesting violations of human rights. Later it established a group to investigate the violations. The General Assembly condemned Chile's violations, as well as her refusal to permit the investigation. See GA Res. 3219 (XXIX), 6 November 1974; GA Res. 32/124, 16 December 1976.

12. Case Concerning the Barcelona Traction, Light and Power Company, Ltd. [1970] I.C.J. paras. 33-34.

13. And "a serious breach on a widespread scale of such obligations" may constitute not merely an international delict but an international crime by the violating state. Article 19, subparagraph 3(c), and commentary, Report of the International Law Commission on the work of its twenty-eighth session, 3 May–23 July 1976, GAOR, Supp. No. 10 (A/31/10) pp. 226 et seq.

14. *See* Ermacora, above note 5.

15. Shachter, *The Twilight Existence of Nonbinding International Agreements,* 71 AM. J. INT'L. L. 296 at 304 (1977).

16. *See,* for example, the Report of the International Law Commission above, note 13 at 227-228, 265-270, and authorities cited therein.

17. ". . . In particular, an essential distinction should be drawn between the obligation of a State towards the international community as a whole, and those arising vis-á-vis another State in the field of diplomatic protection. By their very nature the former are the concern of all States. In view of the importance of the rights involved, all States can be held to have a legal interest in their protection; they are obligations *erga omnes.*

Such obligations derive, for example, in contemporary international law, from the outlawing of acts of aggression, and of genocide, as also from the principles and rules concerning the basic rights of the human person, including protection from slavery and racial discrimination. Some of the corresponding rights of protection have entered into the body of general international law (Reservations to the Convention on the Prevention and Punishment of the Crime of Genocide, Advisory Opinion, I.C.J. Reports 1951, p. 23); others are conferred by international instruments of a universal or quasi-universal character."

Barcelona Traction Case, above note 12, paras. 33–34; *see also* the Report of the International Law Commission, above note 13.

18. The Allied Powers asserted their right to enforce the human rights provisions of World War II peace treaties. Compare the advisory opinion of the International Court of Justice, Interpretation of Peace Treaties with Bulgaria, Hungary and Romania, [1950] I.C.J. 65, 220.

19. Apparently, this general provision was accepted in lieu of an "International Court of Justice" clause (like that in the Genocide Convention), because it was feared that the court's unpopularity might discourage adherence to the covenant.

20. The same implication is to be found in the analogous Article 16 of the International Convention on the Elimination of All Forms of Racial Discrimination.

There is no contrary implication in the fact that state consent to being charged before the Human Rights Committee of the Covenant, whether by other states or by private parties, is optional. (In the Convention on Racial Discrimination, submission to interstate complaint is not optional.) That is a kind of third-party adjudication which has generally required consent, as for the I.C.J.; by contrast, submission to ordinary diplomatic enforcement by the parties is inherent in the international legal system and requires no new consent.

One might argue that International Labor Organization (I.L.O.) Conventions were not intended to be enforceable between the parties; the agreements say nothing of disputes between parties, and I.L.O. Conventions are subject to an elaborate enforcement system linked to each I.L.O. Convention. Perhaps it can be argued, too, that remedies for violation of obligations rooted in the U.N. Charter were intended to be enforced only by the elaborate machinery established by the charter.

21. To the extent that some human rights obligations are not based in international agreement but are deemed now part of customary law (p.3-8 above), perhaps no state could enforce them against another unless the particular obligation were also deemed to be universal, running to all states. Compare above note 13.

22. South West Africa Cases (second phase), [1966] I.C.J. para. 32; compare paras. 34, 50.

This may also be the import of an ambiguous dictum by the International Court of Justice in the Barcelona Traction Case. Having declared that some human rights violations may have become universal and enforceable *erga omnes* (see above note 16), the court said elsewhere in the opinion:

However, on the universal level, the instruments which embody human rights do not confer on States the capacity to protect the victims of infringements of such rights irrespective of their nationality.

The court was apparently saying that the human rights agreements extant today do not create universal obligations enforceable by all states: it was not denying the right of parties to those agreements to enforce them by traditional means for the benefit of their intended beneficiaries.

23. Compare page 27, at note 13, above.

24. It is a nice question whether substantial breach of a human rights agreement by another party, even by all other parties, justifies denunciation or suspension by an innocent party. Compare Vienna Convention on the Law of Treaties, Art. 60 (2)(b). Violation by

one party surely does not warrant others "to retaliate" by violating human rights in turn. But in bilateral agreements, and others that are largely bilateral as between "two sides," is it permissible to threaten retaliation as to certain reciprocal provisions that implicate human rights, in order to deter or undo violations? For example, may State X exclude journalists of State Y if Y excludes her journalists?

25. "Where there is no domestic jurisdiction there is also no problem of intervention." Ermacora, above, note 5, at 431.

26. But *cf.* note 20 above.

27. The West defeated efforts to dilute the domestic jurisdiction clause by replacing it with "internal affairs" or modifying it by "essentially" (which might have also given it a subjective cast).

28. Each succeeding clause is linked to the first by "accordingly," or "likewise:"

They will accordingly refrain from any form of armed intervention or threat of such intervention against another participating State.

They will likewise in all circumstances refrain from any other act of military, or of political, economic or other coercion designed to subordinate to their own interest the exercise by another participating State of the rights inherent in its sovereignty and thus to secure advantages of any kind.

Accordingly, they will, inter alia, refrain from direct or indirect assistance to terrorist activities, or to subversive or other activities directed towards the violent over-throw of the regime of another participating State.

29. Oppenheim, International Law (8th ed. Lauterpacht 1955) 305; Ermacora, above, note 5, at 433. Despite efforts at Helsinki to broaden the sixth principle, the final text uses the legal term "intervention," rather than the broader "interference."

Observations as to the Consequences on the International Plane of Failure to Respect Human Rights

by SUZANNE BASTID

The following observations concern only legal consequences. These depend upon the treaties which bind the states concerned.

In this respect one must distinguish three situations.

1. As between member states of the United Nations who are bound by no other instrument in their mutual relations:

   a. The General Assembly may be appraised of a case in which a failure to respect human rights is invoked. It may order an inquiry, which can only take place on the territory of the state in question with its consent.

   b. If a failure to respect human rights comes within the definition of Resolution 1503 of the Economic and Social Council, the procedure available before the Subcommittee on the Prevention of Discrimination and the Protection of Minorities can now be used. The procedure is confidential in character. Under it, a matter may be sent on to the Human Rights Commission.

2. As between states parties to a multilateral convention defining the rights recognized therein and establishing an appeals procedure, such as the European Convention of Human Rights, the Covenants on Human Rights and the American Convention, defaults may lead to the institution of the conventional procedures provided for. If no recourse is had to these procedures, it would seem that the state in question could object to the use of the general procedures mentioned under I. Only if the special procedures produce no result would recourse to the procedures mentioned under I be justified.

3. The Final Act of Helsinki establishes no remedies with regard to the conduct of signatory states concerning human rights. It provides for a thorough exchange of views at Belgrade on the implementation of the act. A state that is bound by a convention on human rights mentioned under II, and whose attitude with regard to human rights is criticized in the context of the Belgrade conference, might seriously assert that this attitude has not been challenged by the states parties to the convention in question as prescribed by the procedures therein laid down.

4 Obligations Assumed by the Helsinki Signatories

by GÉRARD COHEN JONATHAN
and JEAN-PAUL JACQUÉ

Only after laborious negotiations was the subject of human rights and other humanitarian concerns placed on the agenda of the Conference on Security and Cooperation in Europe that produced the Helsinki Final Act. The Eastern European countries, and particularly the U.S.S.R., wanted the Final Act to concentrate essentially on security matters, and particularly those concerning the inviolability of frontiers and guarantees of peace. Beyond that, these countries would have preferred to deal collectively, under the heading "cooperation," with economic and cultural relations and the environment, limiting pronouncements to rather vague declarations. The Western states, on the other hand, visualized a broader overall program for the improvement of pan-European relations. In their view, any real détente would require a minimum consensus on the development of human rights and, at the very least, a liberalization in the exchange of people and ideas, with the individual being accorded an appropriate place in any new pan-European constitution.

These intentions met with profound hostility from the Eastern countries. They called into question the whole conception of liberty, information, and culture. Whereas, Western society emphasizes the freedom of the individual in his relations with the state, socialist society considers this freedom to be interrelated with the individual's duties to the state and the community. In other words, socialist ideology defines liberty as a nonautonomous value, subordinate to the general interest of socialist society in accordance with values determined by the state. According to this view, for example, pluralism in the field of information should be inadmissable for all practical purposes within a given country, it being understood that journalists have a general duty to support the policy of the state. These conceptions apply to some extent also to literature and art; Eastern countries have an official and conformist art intended to serve the higher social purposes of the state.[1]

In these circumstances, it is understandable that the first reaction of the U.S.S.R. was to rebel against the Western demands for free circulation of information and ideas. This seemed to the Soviets to be a thinly disguised attempt to introduce a "Trojan horse" that would entice citizens away from socialism by propaganda aimed at the internal transformation of the regime.[2] For this reason, the Eastern countries favored an intensification of the exchange of information and ideas, but only those which were connected with "peace and friendship between peoples," to the exclusion of false, "dehumanizing" cultural values. Instead of free circulation, they proposed controlled exchanges, subject to the initiative and approval of official bodies.

They were no less hostile to the idea of the free movement of people. It is no secret that the Eastern countries limit emigration quite strictly. Emigration requests—in particular those made by Jews or political dissidents—are generally followed by discriminatory measures and administrative harassment. "Les autorisations sont souvent refusées ou assorties de taxes si lourdes que la possibilité de sortir en est supprimé."[3] Here again, the U.S.S.R. sought to get away from the idea of freedom of movement by proposing cultural exchanges and contacts between persons controlled by the state.

The West fought stubbornly to overcome this restrictive view of humanitarian cooperation.[4] To counter the argument that their real motive was a desire to undermine the political systems of Eastern states, the Western states insisted that the free circulation of ideas and especially of information is basic to any real "understanding among peoples . . . irrespective of their political, economic and social systems."[5] They maintained that the Soviet approach was purely subjective when it sought to distinguish a priori the values which serve the cause of peace and those they would characterize as dehumanizing. Adults in all countries should be left free to judge competing ideas and to compare information, whatever its origin.[6] Further, the free movement of people could not fail to contribute to "the strengthening of friendly relations and trust among peoples" as well as to the resolution of certain vital humanitarian problems.

Faced with the determination of the Western and neutral states, Mr. Brezhnev was forced to make concessions on this point to ensure that the conference, which he was determined to present as a great success for Soviet multilateral diplomacy, did not fail altogether. As a result, the Eastern bloc agreed to give humanitarian and cultural questions a separate item on the agenda of the conference: this was the origin of Basket III.

EXTENT OF OBLIGATIONS ASSUMED

The provisions of Basket III reflect the nature of the compromise between the two opposing schools of thought. First of all, the final text of Basket III specifies that these undertakings are to be read in the light of the Declaration on Principles Guiding Relations between Participating States set forth in Basket I. This means that the principles of free movement of persons and free circulation of ideas must include respect for the sovereign right of each state to determine its laws and regulations (Principle I), nonintervention in internal affairs (Principle VI), human rights (Principle VII), and the duty to cooperate (Principle IX).

Of greatest importance, in the present context, is Principle VII. It expressly recognizes respect for human rights and singles out some of these rights specifically.[7] Moreover, it contains an important clause providing that the participating states ". . .will also fulfill their obligations as set forth in the international declarations and agreements in this field, including inter alia the International Covenants on Human Rights, by which they may be bound."

Whatever the legal nature of the Final Act, this clause must be interpreted separately. It constitutes a particularly solemn reminder of legal obligations and not of mere resolutions. In fact, many participating states have ratified the European Convention on Human Rights or the United Nations Covenant on Civil and Political Rights, which embody in almost identical terms the right to freedom of expression and information regardless of frontiers, modeled on Article 19 of the Universal Declaration of Human Rights. All these texts contain the three basic elements of freedom of information: the opportunity freely to seek, to receive, and to impart information and opinions. This definition embraces but goes further than that of the traditional freedom of the press and shows that "la protection est étendue à tout le cheminement d'une nouvelle ou d'une opinion, dès son origine à son arrivée au destinataire final, le lecteur, l'auditeur ou le spectateur. La diffusion n'est plus comme jusqu'ici la seule protégée."[8] In it, the notion of freedom of the press has been enlarged and has become a general right to freedom of information. This freedom includes, as the covenant declares, all oral, written, printed, or artistic forms of expression.

Like the Universal Declaration, the covenant provides that the right to freedom of expression and information applies *regardless of frontiers.* This language emphasizes the international dimensions of the right, and its meaning is further clarified by the provisions of the Final Act of the U.N. Conference of 1948. The principle of the free circulation of information also has an indisputable basis in various positive law texts.

Likewise, Article 13 of the Universal Declaration expressly recognizes the right to emigrate. This freedom is embodied in almost identical terms in the International Covenant on Civil and Political Rights (Article 12) and in the European Convention on Human Rights (Protocol 4, Article 2).[9]

All of these texts derive from legal obligations, some of which serve as sources for the provisions of Basket III, which thus constitutes a partial but concrete and, consequently, important implementation of these obligations. In this connection, it should be pointed out that the reference in the Final Act to the Covenant on Civil and Political Rights is doubtless very useful as a minimum standard, but it does not represent the only yardstick for measuring the human rights obligations of the 35 states. The drafting history of Principle VII shows that the states wished to attribute great importance, in the first place, to the Universal Declaration,[10] the escape clauses of which are somewhat less restrictive than those of the covenant, as well as to other more specific, or ultimately more binding, international instruments. However, in the human rights field, a universally accepted principle of interpretation is that, in the case of a multiplicity of applicable rules, the one most favorable to the individual takes precedence.[11]

It should be added, finally, that paragraph 5[12] of Principle VII clearly shows the vital link that exists between détente and respect for human rights. Thus, the undertakings set out in Basket III are designed to achieve a genuine, and not merely a formal, balance between liberty and sovereignty.

Toward this end, the signatory states have decided upon a common program which, without always being as comprehensive[13] as the Western states might have wished, contains some useful provisions concerning the general objective to be attained and the means to be employed to achieve it. The objective is politically very significant, for it seeks:

> to facilitate the freer and wider dissemination of information of all kinds, to encourage cooperation in the field of information and the exchange of information with other countries and to improve the conditions under which journalists from one participating State exercise their profession in another participating State. With regard to human contacts, it is to facilitate free movement and contacts, individually and collectively, whether privately or officially, among persons, institutions and organizations of the participating States, and to contribute to the solution of the humanitarian problems that have arisen in that connection.

For the achievement of these objectives, the states list an action program consisting of a number of measures. Some are quite specific (improvement of working conditions for journalists and lowering of fees for visas) and depend for the most part on unilateral action by states; others are more general (improvement of the dissemination and exchange of information). All presuppose the removal of certain obstacles and depend on a series of practical measures and material arrangements that may be put into effect without too great difficulty, either unilaterally or by agreements between the competent organizations of each country.

Improvement in freedom of information—the most sensitive subject covered in Basket III—could not be expected to be immediate and complete. The aim was to increase the flow of information and related matters.[14] Thus, the states express their intention gradually to increase the quantities and the number of titles of newspapers and publications imported from other states.

To improve access by the public to newspapers and periodicals, they proposed to increase the number of places where these periodicals are on sale and to increase opportunities to subscribe and to read and borrow these publications in libraries. These undertakings are certainly difficult to assess and sometimes ambiguous,[15] but they nevertheless constitute entirely new elements in the East-West dialogue.

In the field of the free movement of persons, the Eastern states, in spite of their international human rights undertakings, were not ready to recognize a general right of emigration. They agreed to facilitate emigration in the context of family reunification or marriage between citizens of different states, and they also agreed to ease restrictions on travel, whatever its purpose.

Agreements such as the Helsinki Final Act, which must deal with these problems as if they existed equally in all the participating states, produce a kind of artificial symmetry. They cannot single out particular states for special attention, yet the situations they address are in fact very unequal: in some countries, the acquisition of books and foreign newspapers, as well as human contacts, are subject to decisions of bodies under the tight control of governmental authorities; in other countries, they depend on very decentralized decisions by individuals or the public as a whole.

Finally, given the reference to Principle I of the "ten commandments" and its echoes in the wording of Basket III, the concept of sovereignty as a bulwark appeared to be so solidly established that the Eastern European states found it possible to accept human rights provisions. It should, nevertheless, be pointed out that the compromise that was achieved leads logically to a limitation upon sovereignty. The Final Act is by no means the embodiment of territorial sovereignty. Its purpose is to enhance cooperation, the avowed common objective. That objective cannot be achieved without some relinquishment of sovereignty.

This result was not at first clearly perceived. Public opinion and the media in Western countries seemed to consider the Final Act a confidence trick by which the U.S.S.R. obtained, at little cost, the legitimization of the territorial and political status quo in Europe in exchange for minor concessions. The reality is, in fact, quite different.

Even in the socialist countries, where the Final Act has been disseminated widely and in its entirety, it has been interpreted by the citizenry as an overall program in which the human rights provisions of Basket III are of the greatest interest. Many people in these countries refer expressly to this text in attempting to initiate various kinds of contacts with the West. The attitude of the Western and neutral states also demonstrates a determination to consider the Final Act an overall program in which all the elements—including the free flow of ideas—are absolutely indivisible.

Détente is a single whole and the application of the texts of Basket III are thus a necessary condition to it. These texts actively refute the selective approach to the various problems suggested by the Eastern states, a method which subordinates the application of provisions aimed at the protection of individuals to the progress of détente between states. The texts also refute the distinction that Mr. Brezhnev attempted to make only a few days after Helsinki, between recommendations of the Final Act which were intended to be immediately applicable and those which were to be acted on only after the conclusion of special agreements between governments, with freedom of information allegedly falling in the latter category. On the contrary, it is generally accepted that, in regard to freedom of information and even more so in regard to human contacts, implementation is to be achieved in large measure by unilateral action.

In fact, what one encounters here is an example of the limits of peaceful coexistence. Mr. Brezhnev stressed (at the Twenty-fifth Congress of the Communist Party of the Soviet Union) that peaceful coexistence concerns relations between states. This, in turn, meant that conflicts between states should not be settled by armed force. But détente in no way abrogates the laws that apply to the class struggle, with the result that, as the East German historian Doernberg puts it, "la lutte idéologique entre les deux systèmes se poursuivra, indépendamment de la création d'un système de sécurité et de coopération en Europe."[16]

But is it not rather paradoxical to affirm a desire for détente while at the same time carrying on a violent ideological struggle? Given this struggle, it is difficult to see how the U.S.S.R., for example, could renounce the tight control it exercises over information disseminated domestically including, of course, information coming from abroad.

This attitude leads the U.S.S.R. to maintain on the domestic plane an intransigent orthodoxy with regard to ideas in general. This orthodoxy is hardly conducive to the penetration of freer information than was previously available on particular aspects of Soviet policy. In fact, the U.S.S.R. continues to view information disseminated from the West to socialist countries as "misinformation" damaging to people and sometimes even as a source of "ideological pollution." This objection, which has also been advanced by other countries such as the German Democratic Republic and Czechoslovakia,[17] was directed in particular at the appeal of Professor Orlov in the Soviet Union and the text of the Charter of 77 in Czechoslovakia.[18]

Thus, although the situation varies in different countries, it should come as no surprise that measures for the improvement of the dissemination of the foreign press has remained mainly symbolic in those countries that have had the most restrictive practices. It is also understandable that what little progress had been made with regard to the working conditions of journalists has recently come almost to a halt.[19]

It is true that opinion in East and West genuinely diverges as to what constitutes the better form of society and government. The Final Act has not ended that ideological debate, yet it should encourage peaceful competition between different ideas based on real knowledge of the society and opinions in each country. Only such interchange of ideas will permit international understanding between peoples, which in turn can only promote more peaceful relations.

Different conceptions of the meaning of détente lead to differing views on the relative importance of the principles stated in the Final Act. The Eastern countries emphasize the principle of sovereignty and nonintervention in internal affairs. In their view, all the other principles are subordinated to and all the parties to the Final Act obligated to maintain a strict respect for the internal rules of each society. In particular, to the Eastern countries cooperation in the humanitarian field means strict respect by the parties for the principle of noninterference in the internal affairs and respect for the laws and administrative regulations in force in these countries. On the other hand, the Western states place heavy emphasis on Principle VII, which deals with human rights and is the basis of Basket III.[20]

Under the Final Act, however, all the principles are of equal value: "All the principles . . . will be equally and unreservedly applied, each of them being interpreted taking into account the others." The Eastern countries must come to understand, therefore, that questions concerning human rights or freedom of movement are not questions which fall solely within the domestic competence of states. Their internationalization permits international debate. It is futile to attempt to mute this debate by the systematic assertion of the principle of nonintervention in internal affairs. That principle must be interpreted by reference to the other provisions of the Final Act, since it is the Final Act in its entirety that states have accepted as governing détente.

LEGAL NATURE OF THE OBLIGATIONS

In analyzing the provisions of the Final Act, we have spoken of "undertakings" and "obligations." Are these terms appropriate? This question goes to the legal nature of the Final Act.[21] It is clear that the Final Act is not a treaty, but rather an agreement, the legal significance of which may vary depending upon a number of considerations.

The Final Act is not an international treaty. For various reasons the states did not desire one and stated so expressly.[22] The final provisions of the Final Act declare that it "is not eligible for registration under Article 102 of the Charter." Similarly, the text of the tenth guiding principle draws a distinction between the obligations of states in law and the application of the provisions drawn up at the conference.

The Final Act, therefore, is an expression of the consent (or intent) of states or what the French would call, "l'accord des volontés." As has been noted, its form is insufficient to determine its legal character. One must proceed to an examination of its content.[23] Some formulations indicate quite strongly the intent (volonté) of the parties. Thus, "the participating States" declare themselves "intending . . . to give full effect to its [Final Act of the conference] results;" they declare their resolve "to pay due regard to and implement the provisions of the Final Act;" and they "declare their determination to act in accordance with the provisions [of the Final Act]."

All of these expressions clearly demonstrate the assent of the states. As J. F. Prévost has ably shown, a declaration of intent is an unequivocal statement of an intention to do or not to do something. It differs from a "wish" which simply states a desire and does not involve any firm intent.[24] More formally, the heads of state and of governments who signed the Final Act all had the "qualité pour representer leur Etat dans les negociations internationales et le cas échéant pour engager sa volonté."[25] Consequently, it is clear that obligations are involved but their effect will vary.

The Helsinki Final Act does not create new and *immediate* legal obligations. It either confirms the existence of preexisting legal obligations, sometimes making them more specific, or it gives rise to moral and political obligations.

A number of provisions, and particularly the guiding principles, are clearly of a legal character. They derive their obligatory force from international custom or from international treaties that gave expression to them: for example, the U.N. Charter, the covenants, and the European Convention on Human Rights. In this respect, Principle VII reiterates the obligations that have been accepted by states in the field of human rights and that have been singled out as constituting the legal basis for the internationally recognized rights of freedom of movement and the free circulation of ideas. Other provisions of the Final Act also embody rules which might already have the status of customary law, at least at the regional level. Their "reaffirmation" in the Final Act removes any ambiguity as to their content and pan-European scope.[26] For example, in the section concerning the working conditions of journalists, the principle of free transmission of information is accepted and "the participating States *reaffirm* that the legitimate pursuit of their professional activity will neither render journalists liable to expulsion nor otherwise penalize them" (emphasis added). Other examples appear in the section relating to human contacts, in particular with regard to several aspects of the concept of reunification of families.

With regard to this category of provisions involving custom or treaties, the Final Act has a legally declaratory effect. Sometimes it adds interesting clarifications, but in the main it manifests the political will of the states to implement their legal obligations.

Actually, the most important characteristic of the Final Act is that it constitutes a moral and political undertaking. This does not mean that its impact is neglible, nor ought it to be criticized on this account by lawyers. Virally has argued very persuasively that moral and political obligations are not necessarily illusory.[27] For example, a moral undertaking is subject to the principle of good faith. A political undertaking, he has said, "est la traduction d'une volonté politique, c'est-à-dire vue résolution ferme; sans elle aucun engagement même régi par le droit, n'a de grandes chances d'être tenu. Mais il est plus que cela car il affecte la situation politique de celui qui le prend, devant l'opinion publique ou vis-à-vis des partenaires politiques ou sur les deux plans."[28] For the defaulting state, the failure to fulfill moral and political obligations would entail a loss of prestige and credibility, resulting in a deterioration in its political relations and thus in détente.

The real question, therefore, is to what extent the provisions of this moral and political undertaking are really binding; that is to say, to what extent the Final Act is drafted "qu'on ne puisse s'en évader à bon compte en se contentant d'un semblant d'exécution."[29] An analysis of the content of the Final Act and particularly of the provisions of Basket III shows that the envisaged measures are sometimes formulated in precise terms. This is the case for some of the rules dealing with the working conditions of journalists or, in the section on human contacts, for the provision under which the participating states "confirm that the presentation of an application for family reunion will not modify the rights and obligations of the applicant or of members of his family."[30]

Finally, the moral and political undertaking might be treated as pre-legal in character. Apparently, also, some of the envisaged "programmatic"[31] acts spelled out in the more precise provisions already contain the psychological element of custom. In itself, this element would be insufficient to create law; but, as it finds its way into the practice of states, it will gradually lead to the legal consolidation of rules.

Whether these pre-legal measures become concrete depends to a large extent upon the way states pursue the follow-up to Helsinki. Serious assessments periodically carried out (committees created to facilitate cooperation with regard to Basket III, for example) would best measure progress. A clearer measure of progress would require the adoption of a more pragmatic approach that avoided a unilateral and global interpretation of détente, such as the U.S.S.R. advances, without embarking on unproductive general discussions of principle. It would be more useful to try to clarify the content of some of the provisions of the Final Act to make them increasingly more binding. In some cases, compliance and implementation time-limits would have to be fixed, since some provisions are vague on this subject. More generally, it would be appropriate to begin gradually to impose express limitations on the right of states to invoke the public order exception as a general escape clause.

In short, a useful result of the Belgrade conference might be an interpretation of some of the general undertakings of the Final Act to make them more concrete and thus to facilitate their implementation. This would be preferable to attempting to give legal force to these obligations because, even if the Final Act became a treaty, its effectiveness would still depend on the precision with which it was drafted and the limitations created by its escape clauses.

IMPLEMENTATION OF THE OBLIGATIONS

The first problem encountered by the signatories to the Final Act concerned how to implement the engagements. Would it be necessary to negotiate point by point or did implementation depend instead upon unilateral measures to be taken by the governments of the states parties?

As noted previously, the Eastern European countries and the Soviet Union took the view that Basket III contained provisions that were to be implemented only by negotiations and international agreements. Besides leading to a selective approach to these problems, this interpretation might have made the application of these provisions of the Final Act subject to the outcome of negotiations and the continual reopening of debates. For this reason, the Western states took the view that, in most cases, the provisions of the Final Act were sufficiently complete to enable implementation by national measures alone.

In fact, in the last part of the Final Act, entitled "Follow-up to the Conference," the participating states declare their resolve, in the period following the Conference, to pay due regard to and implement the provisions of the Final Act of the Conference:

a. unilaterally, in all cases which lend themselves to such action;
b. bilaterally, by negotiations with other participating States;
c. multilaterally, by meetings of experts of the participating States, and also within the framework of existing international organizations, such as the United Nations Economic Commission for Europe and UNESCO, with regard to educational, scientific and cultural cooperation.

In practice, all of these means have been used. Thus, in the field of information, an exchange of notes has taken place to allow the application of some provisions of the Final Act. In other cases, domestic regulation of a matter has sufficed. At the level of domestic regulation, some measures have been taken unilaterally; while, in other cases, notably those concerning the movement of diplomats, appropriate regulations have been adopted simultaneously by the U.S. and the U.S.S.R. Reciprocity, in this case at least, expresses a tacit agreement between the states concerned. Sometimes the implementing measures did not have to be taken by governmental organs as, for example, in the case of agreements between editors cr between television networks. Finally, particularly in the cultural field, implementation has also been the subject of decisions taken within the UNESCO framework.

As far as accomplishments are concerned, particular attention should be paid to the fields of human contacts and the circulation of information. It is not that cooperation in the cultural and educational fields is of secondary importance, but that the spirit of Helsinki has manifested itself more slowly in this context. In fact, this part of the Final Act constitutes a long-term program of action and, unlike other parts of Basket III, does not call for any practical steps to be taken immediately. In addition, cultural cooperation is already well developed and is the fruit of existing bilateral agreements. Gradually, as new agreements are concluded, the effects of the Final Act can be measured. Negotiations are in progress in the publishing field, the translation of works is increasing, and exchanges in the field of education are taking place more frequently. In addition, at its General Conference held in Nairobi in 1976, UNESCO adopted a three-year program for European cooperation and acted upon a number of recommendations contained in the Final Act (including a contribution to the creation of a cultural data bank and to a calendar of cultural events in Europe).

The accomplishments in the area of human contacts and the circulation of information are on the whole minimal, and vary from country to country. Seemingly, the passage of time produced a gradual weakening of the positive effects of the Final Act, an impression that emerges from the latest report of the American administration to the U.S. Commission on Security and Cooperation in Europe. In our opinion, the rapid implementation of a number of concrete measures provided for in the Final Act obscured the differences of opinion that existed on many substantive issues. After the initial optimism which accompanied the first steps towards implementation, the basic disagreements again surfaced, which suggests that one of the aims of the Belgrade conference should be to devise new and concrete measures to make it possible to proceed with the implementation of the Final Act. The unevenness of the results should remind us that the Helsinki conference was not a negotiation among mere states but among "sovereign and independent states." It would, thus, be contrary to the spirit of the Final Act to view its implementation as a confrontation between the East and West. Problems relating to the implementation of the Final Act must instead be confronted by each of the signatories.[32]

Human Contacts

The Final Act attempts to establish the freer movement of persons, as provided in Article 12 of the International Covenant on Civil and Political Rights. The provisions on human contacts derive either from humanitarian considerations (contacts between members of the same family, reunification of families, and marriage between citizens of different states) or from a desire to facilitate contacts between nationals of the East and West (travel for personal or professional reasons, improvement of conditions for tourism, meetings among young people, and sports events).

A reading of the Final Act shows that, in this field, the drafters opted for measures which impress upon the signatories the necessity for conducting themselves in accordance with "the spirit of Helsinki" and that repeatedly remind them what their conduct should be. Thus, the signatories "undertake to examine favourably" or "deal in a positive and humanitarian spirit" with the applications presented to them. Although the wording used does not imply an obligation to adopt new domestic regulations, it clearly assumes the subjective acceptance by the signatories of limitations upon their discretionary conduct.

However, where it has been possible to agree upon the need to remove particular obstacles, these obstacles are mentioned expressly, with the result that the rules provided for in the Final Act can be given direct internal effect by domestic legislation incorporating them. This is true of the fee schedule for visas and provisions concerning the renewal of visa applications that had been previously refused. In these cases, the specific undertakings of the Final Act have generally been followed by domestic implementing measures.

Reunification of families. The Final Act provides that applications for emigration visas be dealt with in a positive and humanitarian spirit, and it establishes a number of practical measures designed to facilitate the application process.

The most important development to date is the German-Polish agreement which provides for the return to the Federal Republic of Germany of people of German origin. There are, according to some estimates, about 125,000 such persons. This agreement was concluded on August 2, 1975, in exchange for financial benefits. Although it was not linked to the implementation of the Final Act and grew out of the specific relations existing between Poland and the Federal Republic of Germany, this agreement, given the context of Helsinki, is nonetheless evidence of a climate of détente.

Other population movements involve Germany for the most part: from the German Democratic Republic to the Federal Republic of Germany, from Czechoslovakia to the Federal Republic, or from the Soviet Union to the Federal Republic. The reunification of families is also one of the themes of Soviet emigration to Israel because it provides one of the few justifications for emigration visas to Israel. It is interesting to note that emigration visas for Israel may be issued to non-Jewish dissidents who have not applied for them. This attitude of the Soviet authorities has been much criticized as an attempt to establish a link between dissidence in general and the desire to emigrate to Israel.

Some governments refuse authorization to emigrate if the request is to rejoin a member of the family who has left the country without authorization and who is, therefore, considered an illegal emigrant. This is the case in Czechoslovakia, where one applicant for a visa received the following reply from the competent government department:

> The denial by the Regional Passport and Visa Office was based on paragraph 4, item 1, letter (a) of Public Law No. 63/1965/Sv concerning travel documents and paragraph 1, letter (b) of the Government Ruling No. 114/1969/Sv and is therefore fully justified. According to these rules it is contrary to the State's interest to allow Czechoslovak citizens long-term private sojourns abroad, and that includes emigration. Apart from that, in your case, it is also based on the fact that you would be emigrating to join Czechoslovak citizens who are residing abroad without the permission of Czechoslovak authorities.[33]

Such a policy, particularly as it is applied in Czechoslovakia, must restrict favorable consideration of visa applications.

On the whole, the Eastern countries demonstrate an important evolution only in principles. In practice, authorizations are granted on the basis of subjective criteria and no real law of family reunification exists. In fact, because the governmental authorities in the East have not agreed in the Final Act to recognize this right,[34] the only measures taken to implement it were to simplify the application procedure for visas or to lower their cost. Thus, in the Soviet Union, the following very positive practical measures have actually been taken:

a. The cost of emigration visas has been lowered from 400 to 300 rubles as of January 1, 1976;
b. The number of necessary favorable recommendations in support of an emigration application has been reduced;
c. Fees will be levied only on applications for emigration which are accepted and not on those which are refused;
d. An application which has been refused may be renewed six months after the refusal (previously, the waiting time had been a year);
e. Finally, children under sixteen years may now travel on their parents' passports.

This set of measures makes emigration less expensive and allows the applicant to renew his application frequently and at lower cost. These measures were expressly provided for in the Final Act and constitute a direct application of it.

On the other hand, the taxes on gifts coming from the West have been increased from 100 percent to 600 percent. This increase in customs duties has an indirect effect on some of those potential emigrants who have lost their jobs because of their applications to emigrate and who are relying, in part at least, upon gifts from the West to support their needs. In fact, no significant improvement is noticeable in the position of these individuals. Although the Final Act provides that the rights and duties of emigration applicants will not be affected by an application to emigrate, this obligation is apparently not being strictly complied with.[35]

The practice relating to temporary family visits varies. The Final Act provides that applications be examined favorably and that no distinction be made based on the country of origin or destination. It also provides that documents be issued within reasonable time limits and be given priority treatment in cases of urgent necessity. The fees to be demanded must be "acceptable."

Reference has already been made to the Czech situation, where even temporary exit visas are refused to Czech nationals who wish to visit members of their families who have left the country illegally. But the major movement-of-family problems affect relations between the two Germanys. Here, although the number of journeys from the German Democratic Republic to the Federal Republic has increased, in particular for family reasons, the inverse movement is greater. However, the East German authorities have taken measures which interfere with travel. A 24-hour visa has been instituted for visits to East Berlin by people who are not of German origin. Germans who have left the German Democratic Republic have been refused permission to re-enter the country to rejoin their families even though they have the necessary documents.

As to the provisions of the Final Act designed to facilitate marriages between nationals of different countries, specific trends are difficult to discern. Observers have the impression that no clear doctrine exists on the subject, but that some ad hoc measures are being taken. Sometimes, following spectacular publicity, an authorization is granted, but on the whole no definite improvement is apparent. Romania has attempted to justify its restrictive attitude towards such marriages by pointing to the number of disillusioned spouses returning from Western countries.

Other human contacts.   In the area of other human contacts, no significant improvements are discernible. Although the Eastern countries have provided statistics showing a very extensive movement by tourists of their nationality, these figures usually reflect not only East-West tourism but also tourism among the Eastern countries, which is, of course, much more common.

Travel for personal or professional reasons is not always authorized. Minor agreements have been concluded, such as one between the United States and Czechoslovakia that is designed to eliminate restrictions on travel by diplomats and especially on the designation of obligatory entry points. However, for the time being, the Soviet Union has apparently not accepted the American proposal for granting multiple entry visas to businessmen and students residing in the Soviet Union for substantial periods of time. On the contrary, new visa regulations for businessmen shorten the duration of visas and require businessmen to declare their itinerary outside the Soviet Union. Travel permits have sometimes been refused. The best known cases involve the authors Vachav Havel and Pavel Kouhout, who were refused the right to attend the first performance of their work abroad. The poet and song-writer Wolf Birmann was the victim of another kind of practice: his citizenship in the German Democratic Republic was withdrawn while he was on a business trip in the Federal Republic. In the United States, restrictions have been placed on the entry of foreign trade union representatives. President Carter has decided to lift these restrictions.

As for tourism, the U.S. and Soviet governments have been discussing ways to reduce the number and size of areas that are off-limits to tourists. Similarly, the U.S. government has proposed to the Eastern countries a reciprocal reduction in the cost of tourist visas. The Eastern countries emphasize the time that it takes to obtain visas for Western countries and the difficulties involved in making certain visits, particularly to factories. With regard to the latter complaint, the Western states can do little more than to suggest that travel agencies organize such visits. Concerning the issuance of exit visas, the practice of the Polish, Yugoslav, and Hungarian authorities is very positive. Of all the Eastern countries, these three have permitted the greatest number of tourist journeys to the West. On the other hand, Romania has expressed concern over the number of Romanian tourists who have not returned (10 percent to 15 percent of the visas granted) and is reducing considerably the number of exit visas that are granted. Of course, the conceptions regarding the nature of tourism differ. The Eastern European countries and the U.S.S.R. prefer trips by official delegations or, at least, trips organized and controlled by government authorities, while the Western countries would prefer an increase in travel by relatively unsupervised or uncontrolled tourists.

The major difference between the East and the West relates to the right of individuals to leave their country and to return. The Eastern countries are willing to accept an easing of the formalities applicable to foreign travel, but they do not want to recognize foreign travel as a *right*. They insist upon retaining discretion to grant or to refuse visas. On the other hand, appreciable progress in reducing these formalities has been achieved or is being achieved and was one of the goals of the Final Act. The parties have attempted to fulfill the specific and concrete undertakings which they accepted, but they are not going further than that. At Belgrade it might, therefore, be desirable to identify some new points on which all parties could agree that progress could be made.

Circulation of Information

Concerning the circulation of information, the differences between signatories of the Final Act were the most pronounced, centering on the content of the information to be circulated and the means of circulation. It is not surprising that divergences have appeared in the interpretation and implementation of the Final Act.

Improvement in the circulation, access to, and exchange of information. Since its inception, UNESCO has been pursuing the goals which the parties to the Final Act set themselves in the field of information. The organization has contributed to the conclusion of legal instruments designed to facilitate the free circulation of information. The conventions concluded under the auspices or at the initiative of UNESCO constitute a multilateral framework for the complete achievement of the goals articulated in the Final Act.

It is true that the Florence and Beirut conventions, of December 3, 1958, (concluded under the auspices of UNESCO) on the exchange of official publications and the exchange of publications in general, have only a limited scope. They permit the exchange of documents that are not made available to the public except through libraries or official institutions. But they abolish customs duties and quantitative restrictions on books and other publications, and they facilitate the importation of educational, scientific, and cultural audiovisual material. Broadly complementary, these two conventions to a large extent eliminate customs duties, or even currency restrictions, on the free circulation of information. They both contain a "public order" reservation. The ratification of these two UNESCO conventions by all the parties to the Helsinki Final Act would be an important contribution to the circulation of information. Political obstacles would certainly still remain, but a number of practical difficulties could thereby be overcome.

Regarding the dissemination of written information, the measures taken have varied greatly from country to country. The Soviet Union imports only a limited number of foreign periodicals: 40 copies of *Le Monde* and the *London Times* and 60 copies of the *International Herald Tribune*. These periodicals are made available to tourists in the hotels of Moscow and of some larger cities. The practice of the German Democratic Republic is similar; *Le Monde* estimates that it has only three subscribers there. On the other hand, Hungary and Czechoslovakia[36], according to estimates by Radio Free Europe, import the largest number of Western publications per inhabitant. The Polish practice is interesting in that foreign publications are widely imported and made available to the public in international press clubs.

The goal of free circulation is, thus, far from being fully realized with regard to either periodicals or books. The authorities in the East refuse to allow the organization of exhibitions of Western books unless they can control the works to be displayed.

In the audiovisual field, cooperation is mainly the outgrowth of bilateral agreements on cultural cooperation. These agreements provide for exchanges of radio and television broadcasts, for the presentation of films, and even for the joint production of commercial films.

Commercial agreements concluded between television networks have resulted in the transmission of broadcasts. Regular exchanges of information take place between Eurovision and Intervision. But all activities remain subject to state control. The cultural agreements provide that the texts of broadcasts exchanged must be communicated in advance and that, in all cases the state retains the right not to transmit any broadcast if its content would prejudice friendship between peoples.

The Final Act contains little more than a discreet allusion to the jamming of radio broadcasts:

> The participating States note the expansion in the dissemination of information broadcast by radio, and express the hope for the continuation of this process, so as to meet the interest of mutual understanding among peoples and the aims set forth by this Conference.

This text is ambiguous and can be read in two ways. It states the principle of free dissemination but, according to the Soviet Union, the principle must be used to promote mutual understanding between peoples and the goals of the Helsinki conference. Thus, it is hardly surprising that the Soviets feel that some broadcasts are contrary to the spirit of Helsinki and declare that the very existence of Radio Liberty and Radio Free Europe is a violation of the act to the extent that these stations transmit "criminal" or "warlike" information. Radio Liberty is jammed in the Soviet Union. Bulgaria and Czechoslovakia jam Radio Free Europe, and Poland jams it occasionally. The Voice of America has not been jammed since 1973, but it continues to be vigorously criticized. The decision of President Carter to strengthen VOA's transmitters will only revive the dispute in this field. The practice of the Soviet Union and the Eastern countries leads one to ask whether, beyond the provisions of the Final Act, jamming is prohibited by general international law. In the framework of the International Telecommunication Union, the Torremolinos Convention regulates the assignment of frequencies so as to avoid interference. Frequencies properly registered have a right to protection against interference under the regulation applicable to radio communications, which regulation also prohibits the transmission of superfluous signals. In our view, jamming is a voluntary interference that can be characterized as the transmission of superfluous signals from authorized transmitters. But the regulation applicable to radio communications is not universally accepted; the Soviet Union, in particular, has ratified the Torremolinos Convention with reservation as to these regulations. On the level of general international law, the U.N. General Assembly, in 1950, condemned jamming, citing the principles of freedom of information and the right of the individual to be fully informed without regard to national frontiers. Of course, at that time, the majority of the General Assembly was very different from the present majority. In this respect, much depends on whether support exists for a general principle of free international circulation of information. If this principle is accepted, then jamming would clearly conflict with it.

In the Soviet view, the information sector as a whole is marked by an imbalance, in that the amount of time and space devoted by the Eastern media to information from the West is greater than that accorded by Western media to information from the East. In addition, the information selected by the West is not always that which the East would like. According to the East, demonstrations of dissidents are emphasized by the West at the expense of substantive information on the realities of life in the Eastern countries. In addition, the Western commercial system does not always accord the literary, cinematographic, and television productions from the East the importance that the East deems its productions deserve. Finally, an imbalance exists in the exchanges of information between Intervision and Eurovision for the most part, to the detriment of Intervision.

This situation results from the differences between the two information systems; one is governmental in character and the other is commercial. To bring about a change would require increased government direction and control over the media by the West, which would conflict with the Western conception of freedom of information. This is one of the reasons why, in Nairobi, the West opposed the UNESCO draft declaration on mass communication. The draft included a provision making states responsible for the activities of the mass communication media within their jurisdictions, which implied state control over the content of information disseminated by the media.

However, the differences as to the meaning of freedom of information should not serve as a pretext to escape obligations assumed in the Final Act. The states parties must, at the very least, ensure that their domestic legislation poses no obstacles to the free circulation of information. Toward this goal, they have also assumed a duty to promote action by private persons and institutions and to foster other initiatives.

Improvement of Working Conditions of Journalists

The provisions in the Final Act dealing with journalists fix specific objectives that have been partially achieved. Following an exchange of notes between the U.S. and the U.S.S.R., one of the first measures taken in application of the Final Act was to grant multiple entry and exit visas for journalists. The U.S.S.R. also accorded journalists travel privileges comparable to those enjoyed by diplomats. Finally, foreign journalists in the U.S.S.R. may now deal directly with various government authorities without having to use the Ministry for Foreign Affairs as an intermediary. The Final Act also provides that journalists be allowed to import professional material and equipment temporarily. This provision has already been implemented by those parties to the Final Act who have ratified the Convention on the Temporary Importation of Technical Materials. Concluded under the auspices of UNESCO and the Council on Customs Cooperation, this convention applies particularly to journalists and considerably simplifies customs formalities.

The improvements brought about through implementation of the Final Act should not be permitted to obscure the unsatisfactory status of journalists. Refusals of visas are not uncommon and expulsion may be ordered without the possibility of appeal.[37] The expulsion of George Krimsky, an Associated Press correspondent, was apparently motivated by his contacts with the dissident group organized around Professor Orlov, even though Krinsky was officially attacked for violating a Soviet law that prohibits using foreign currency to pay for the services of Soviet citizens. A New York Times correspondent was arrested in Czechoslovakia and expelled without being allowed to contact his embassy. In addition to the threat of expulsion, the work of press correspondents is made more difficult because they may be castigated by name in the Soviet press for their articles. This publicity, in turn, may produce "spontaneous" demonstrations by Soviet citizens expressing their disapproval. Steps have also been taken to intimidate Soviet citizens who have had contacts with foreign correspondents or to intimidate the correspondents themselves, who may be summoned by the Soviet authorities and chastized for the content of their articles. The measures taken under the Final Act have settled some important technical questions, but they leave unresolved the fundamental problem: the freedom of the foreign correspondent to exercise his profession.

Examination of the provisions relating to human contacts and to information shows that, in the two years since the Final Act was signed, some progress has been achieved. But this progress relates only to certain concrete matters mentioned specifically in the Final Act. Moreover, fundamental differences remain on the major issues: free movement of persons and free circulation of information.

The Helsinki Act is a very rich "code" on European co-operation. It had always been understood that its application would be very gradual and that progress would not be spectacular. Its uniform interpretation will take time, but to achieve this result is the purpose of the long-term negotiations now being organized. At the Belgrade conference, a first assessment will be made. Judging from their statements,[38] the Western states at the time of the present writing do not intend to turn this review into a tribunal. They will strongly insist, however, that the assessment cover all the provisions of the Final Act, including those of Basket III.

Experience shows, however, that because of the ideological differences between the parties, progress can be achieved only with regard to clearly defined and limited issues; obligations drafted in general terms will be interpreted in contradictory ways. It can also be readily predicted that, because of the use made of Basket III by some western states, the eastern European countries and the Soviet Union are unlikely to favor expansion of the Basket III commitments. The only reasonable way to proceed is by small steps. The over-all objectives of the Final Act can only be achieved by concentrating on short-term goals. Only the implementation of specific obligations provides a meaningful standard for measuring the effectiveness of the progress being achieved in the implementation of the Final Act. It would, therefore, be useful if, among other things, the Belgrade conference produced more concrete reformulations of some of the general obligations contained in the Final Act. This would facilitate the implementation of these obligations.

Be that as it may, the western states must reiterate that détente cannot be divorced from progress accomplished in humanitarian cooperation and human rights. It is precisely with regard to this section of the Final Act, which was inspired by their initiative, that the western states expect from their co-signatories some tangible evidence of good will, so as to expand and promote détente which, in turn, will inevitably lead to revisions of overrigid conceptions of sovereignty.

NOTES

1. Official bodies (Union of Writers, Union of Artists) control productions and play a political role. Symptomatic in this regard is the statement of the Soviet writer Kornejchouk "Par notre oeuvre, nous défendons notre gouvernement, notre parti, notre peuple . . . Comment pouvons-nous, écrivains soviétiques, ne pas être aussi des soldats." ("By our work, we defend our government, our party, our people. . . . How can we, soviet writers, avoid being soldiers, too?") From Depuy, *La protection et les limites de la liberté d'expression de l'artiste dans la société européene,* (REVUE DES DROITS DE L'HOMME at 49 (1974)).

2. In Rude Pravo (February 10, 1972), for example, the following statement appears: "Il n'est pas difficile de déduire que [la libre circulation des idées] c'est là le cheval de Troie que l'Ouest essaie d'introduire clandestinement dans toutes les proches négociations entre les pays européens . . . C'est un cheval de Troie employé comme l'instrument de subversion contre les pays socialistes." ("It is not difficult to deduce that [the free circulation of ideas] is a Trojan horse that the West is trying to introduce surreptitiously into all future negotiations between European countries . . . . This Trojan horse is being used as a subversive instrument against all socialist countries.")

3. "The authorizations are often refused, or burdened by such heavy taxes that any real possibility of leaving the country is greatly reduced." Chappez, *Les problèmes de la troisième Corbeille de la Conférence de sécurité et la coopération en Europe,* INSTITUT INTERNATIONAL DES DROITS DE L'HOMME 7ême session d'enseignement, Strasbourg (July 5-30, 1976).

4. Manin, *La Conférence sur la sécurité et la coopération en Europe*, NED at 42 (March 15, 1976), No. 4271–4272.

5. Preamble to the third chapter of the Final Act.

6. Andreani, *La Conférence sur la sécurité et la coopération en Europe, in* REGIONALISME ET UNIVERSALISME DANS LE DROIT INTERNATIONAL CONTEMPORAIN, at 122 (1977).

7. The content of Principle VII will not be examined in detail, since it will be discussed in other chapters (notably chapter 5). It should be noted that the rights specifically mentioned are subject to no reservation.

Some speakers wondered whether the list of Human Rights expressly stated in Principle VII should be extended. At this time, we do not share this point of view. It would be premature to amend the Final Act and, as will be explained below, it would be preferable for the time being to harmonize the interpretation of the present provisions and to attempt to translate them into concrete form.

8. "protection is now extended to the channeling of news or opinion from origin to final destination: the reader, listener, or spectator. The dissemination of news is no longer the only aspect protected." BARRELET, LA LIBERTE DE L'INFORMATION, at 47 (1972).

9. Similarly, these texts require respect for family unity.

10. The eighth paragraph reads:

> in the field of human rights and fundamental freedoms, the participating States will act in conformity with the purpose and principles of the Charter of the United Nations and with the Universal Declaration of Human Rights. They will *also* fulfill their obligations as set forth in the international declarations and agreements in this field, including inter alia the International Covenants on Human Rights, by which they may be bound (emphasis added).

The word "also" seems to show that the position given to the covenant is neither exclusive nor privileged. It will be noted that the expression "obligation" may refer to the provisions of the Universal Declaration (listed on the same footing as the U.N. Charter) as well as to the provisions of the covenant.

11. Cohen Jonathan, *Les rapports entre la Convention européenne des droits de l'homme et le Pacte des Nations-Unies sur les droits civils et politiques, in* REGIONALISME ET UNIVERSALISME DANS LE DROIT INTERNATIONAL CONTEMPORAIN, at 321 (1977).

12. "The participating States recognise the universal significance of human rights and fundamental freedoms, respect for which is an essential factor for the peace, justice and well-being necessary to ensure the development of friendly relations and cooperation among themselves as among all States."

13. The problem of the jamming of radio broadcasts, for example, is not the subject of any particular provisions.

14. Chappez, above, note 3.

15. Already certain commentators in Eastern countries are arguing that the free flow of information applies only to information which contributes to "the development of mutual understanding between the participating States". The restrictiveness and the ambiguities are even more evident to broadcast information. "The participating States note the expansion in the dissemination of information broadcast by radio, and express the hope for the continuation of this process, so as to meet the interest of mutual understanding among peoples and the aims set forth by this Conference."

16. "The ideological struggle between the two systems will continue, whether or not a system of security and cooperation is created in Europe." Cited by Charvin: *La Souveraineté et la Conférence sur la sécurité et la coopération en Europe,* MELANGES OFFERTS À GEORGE BURDEAU at 1028 (1977).

17. At a recent meeting in Belgrade of 90 representatives of the European press, Mr. Kubin of Rude Pravo, Prague, expressed his indignation at the "misinformation" propagated in the West against his country: "Les journalistes étrangers," he said in particular, are seeking contacts with "groupuscules qui ne représentent rien, au lieu de s'adresser aux sources serieuses d'informations qui sont à leur disposition." ("Foreign journalists," he said in particular, are seeking contacts with "small groups representative of nobody, instead of making use of the serious sources of information which are at their disposal.") (Le Monde, April 29, 1977).

18. As Mr. Ghebali replied, criticisms concerning the quality of information disseminated by the Western media are justified to the extent that the media are critical of their own governments as well as of foreign governments. "Les gouvernements de l'Ouest

ne pourront par conséquent améliorer la qualité de l'information sur l'Est qu'au prix d'un contrôle contre lequel ils s'insurgent par principe et dont ils dénoncent précisément les effets néfastes pour l'individu." ("Therefore, the Western governments will be unable to improve the balance of information disseminated from the East unless they submit to censorship, to which they are opposed in principle and which would result in deprivation of individual rights.") *Le bilan intermédiaire de la CSCE à la veille de Belgrade*, politique étrangère (May 1977). It matters little if the Eastern countries import a great quantity of information, particularly televised, from the West if this material is selected by the government. The objective set in the Final Act is to achieve not only a wider but a freer circulation of information.

19. In its Resolution 654 (1977) on the implementation of the Final Act, the Parliamentary Assembly of the Council of Europe deplored "setbacks in the process initiated after 1 August 1975 whose aim was to facilitate the work of foreign correspondents." Doc. AS/Inf. (77) 9/8.

20. The Eastern states also emphasize Principles IX (cooperation among states) and X (fulfillment in good faith). Parliamentary Assembly to the Council of Europe, Report of Mr. Aubert on the political importance of the Final Act and the principles governing relations between the participating States. Council of Europe, Doc. 3951 (28.3.1977).

21. Cohen Jonathan, *Liberté de Circulation des Informations et Souveraineté des Etats,* General report presented to Societe Français pour le Droit International (June 2, 1977).

22. Andreani, above, note 6, at 114. Some small states have regretted this.

23. Virally, *La Décennie pour le développement,* Annuaire Français de Droit International, at 26 (1970).

24. Prévost, *Observations sur la nature juridique de l'Acte Final,* Annuaire Français de Droit International, at 148 (1975).

25. "necessary status to represent their governments in international negotiations, and to express their intent [volonté]." *Id.*, at 145.

26. It seems that certain Soviet lawyers, such as Tumkin, have understood the Helsinki Final Act to indicate that at least some international customs or some principles of international law should be applied on a pan-European level.

27. Virally, above note 23, at 29.

28. "is the expression of a political intent [volonté]; that is to say, a firm decision. Absent such firm intent, no legal obligation has any chance of being kept. Yet it is more than that, for its public expression affects the political position of the maker of the statement, in relation to public opinion or with respect to political relationships, or both." *Id.*, at 30.

29. "so that one cannot escape its obligations merely by giving the appearance of compliance." *Id.*, at 31.

30. *Id.*

31. *Id.*

32. To assess the state of implementation, the following documents have for the most part been used: Committee on International Relations, U.S. House of Representatives, First Semi-Annual Report by the President to the Commission on Security and Cooperation in Europe (1976); Committee on International Relations, U.S. House of Representatives, Second Semi-Annual Report of the President to the Commission on Security and Cooperation in Europe (1977); *Debate on Implementation of the Final Act of the Conference on Security and Cooperation in Europe,* Eur. Consult. Ass. Deb., AS/inf. (77) at 9; Segre, *The Application of the Final Act of the CSCE,* report to the 23rd ordinary session of the WEU Assembly, Doc. 732, May 9, 1977; Ghebali, *Le bilan intérimaire de la CSCE à la veille de Belgrade,* Politique etrangere, at 109-153 (1977). With the exception of those of the Council of Europe (which contain a report on the position of all member states), these documents confine their assessment to the implementation of the Final Act by the U.S.S.R. and the Eastern countries.

33. Council of Europe, Doc. AS/inf. 77/9, at 114.

34. No agreement exists on the concept of family unity or the definition of what constitutes a family.

35. According to the Soviet authorities, 98 percent of applications for emigration by Soviet Jews have been accepted. It is difficult, however, to put a figure to the number of applications that have not been made because the potential applicants fear that their position will be aggravated by placing an application.

36. Czechoslovakia has, however, recently reduced imports of foreign periodicals.

37. The Final Act provides that a journalist must be informed of the reasons for his expulsion and be afforded the opportunity to submit an application for the reexamination of his case.

38. *See,* for example, the conclusion "Looking Toward Belgrade" of the second American report to the CSCE Commission. "While we have no desire to see the Belgrade meeting devolve into an exchange of recriminations and polemics, we believe a full and frank review of implementation, as mandated by the Final Act, should remain the central task of the Belgrade conference." See also Resolution 654 (1977) of the Parliamentary Assembly of the Council of Europe, para. 43, which "Regards the Belgrade meetings as a stage in a long-term process enabling, *in an atmosphere devoid of polemics,* a preliminary review to be made of the Helsinki agreements which, in accordance with the idea of international cooperation, are based on mutual concessions and advantages" (emphasis added).

5 The Interrelationship between the Helsinki Final Act, the International Covenants on Human Rights, and the European Convention on Human Rights

by JOCHEN ABR. FROWEIN

GENERAL REMARKS

According to the International Court of Justice, in the *Barcelona Traction* case, the principles and rules concerning basic human rights create obligations *erga omnes*. This could be regarded as a recognition of the postwar developments that have taken place in this important field of international law.[1] Although it is not clear whether the Court also had in mind the International Covenants on Human Rights (which had not, at that time, entered into force), there is a strong presumption to that effect. No other general instruments on the universal level exist apart from the Universal Declaration, but the Court spoke of "instruments," so it is difficult to imagine that it meant only the Universal Declaration.[2] However, this recognition statement was connected with a far-reaching statement emphasizing that universal human rights instruments do not empower states parties to protect the victims of human rights violations irrespective of their nationality.[3] From that angle, the surprising and, at first sight, progressive reference to human rights in the judgment would appear to have some rather dangerous aspects. Human rights guarantees which cannot be protected by some action, however weak, are not worth the ink with which they are written.

The following remarks explore the present status of the human rights issue and the interrelationship between the universal instruments, the Helsinki Final Act, and the European Convention on Human Rights. Perhaps Helsinki should be regarded as one more step towards a general recognition that human rights are a legitimate issue of international concern. Nevertheless, the Final Act is not a binding legal instrument; that fact has been expressed in its text in several ways.[4] However, the absence of legal force does not negate the legal relevance of the document. International law has always been influenced by declarations which were not legally binding as such.[5] For example, resolutions and declarations of the U.N. General Assembly have considerably influenced discussions and legal arguments concerning the development of international law.[6]

In analyzing the significance of the Final Act, one should distinguish several different situations. First, the Final Act may illuminate the understandings of its signatories regarding their obligations under general or specific international law.[7] Second, the wording of the Final Act might, at the very least, show that some areas — in this instance, human rights — are not exclusively within the domestic jurisdiction of states.[8] Third, an instrument that is not legally binding, may be used to interpret an instrument that is binding.[9]

THE GENERAL RELATIONSHIP OF THE HELSINKI FINAL ACT AND THE HUMAN RIGHTS INSTRUMENTS

It is of some importance that, in dealing with human rights, the Declaration on Guiding Principles proclaimed in the Helsinki Final Act contains a special reference to other human rights instruments. In the last paragraph of Principle VII, the participating states declare their willingness to conform with the purposes and principles of the U.N. Charter and with the Universal Declaration of Human Rights. Note that the Universal Declaration appears to be placed on the same level as the U.N. Charter. This will certainly strengthen the growing tendency to treat the Universal Declaration as part of general international law.[10]

Apart from strengthening the Universal Declaration, the Final Act may provide some guidelines for the interpretation of the International Covenants. This could be significant, especially with regard to the detailed provisions set out in the section on Cooperation in Humanitarian and Other Fields (Basket III). A few examples might clarify the application of the Basket III proposition. Article 19 of the International Covenant on Civil and Political Rights guarantees the right to freedom of expression and freedom to seek information. Chapter 2 of Basket III contains rather detailed statements on the improvement of the flow of information between the participating states. The argument that Article 19 of the International Covenant does not cover foreign newspapers (an argument which is hardly tenable given the wording of the article) could certainly not be validly asserted among the states participating in the Final Act. These states have agreed to the principle of cooperation in the Field of Information.[11] A similar argument applies to the provision on the protection of the family, found in Article 23 of the International Covenant. The right to marry, as guaranteed in the covenant, must be read to include the right to marry a citizen from another participating state, as is recognized in the chapter on Human Contacts found in Basket III of the Final Act.

Article 26 of the International Covenant on Civil and Political Rights contains the principle of equality before the law. Article 27 protects ethnic, religious, or linguistic minorities, but this protection is limited to the areas of culture, religion, and language. Equality before the law, as enunciated in Article 26, is not specifically stated to apply to members of a minority. Of course, we are inclined to take that consequence for granted, viewing the relationship between Article 26 and Article 27 as that of a general clause followed by a specific clause providing additional protection. But in fact, the treatment of minorities is not always in conformity with this understanding. In defending a practice denying minorities equality before the law, an argument could be made that Article 27 restricts the meaning of Article 26, thus denying minorities the latter's protection. Such an argument would be impossible under Guiding Principle VII, paragraph 4, of the Final Act. This principle expressly guarantees equality before the law to minorities.

The contention that account should be taken of the Final Act when interpreting the International Covenants cannot be easily justified by reference to the rules of interpretation in the Vienna Convention on the Law of Treaties. The Final Act is neither a rule of international law within the meaning of Article 31(3)(c) of the Vienna Convention, nor a "subsequent practice in the application of the treaty'' as specified in Article 31(3)(b). Under specific conditions, it may be possible, however, to treat the Final Act as an agreement in a nontechnical sense, according to the application of the provisions of the Human Rights Covenants as specified in Article 31(3)(a) of the Vienna Convention. More important, the consensus of the states on human rights, as declared in the Final Act, must be considered when the object and purpose of the International Covenants are interpreted in accordance with Article 31, paragraph 1, of the Vienna Convention.

Later developments in the protection of human rights help to clarify the object and purpose of the International Covenants on specific matters. Human rights instruments, in particular, cannot be interpreted only in the context of the historic situation that existed when these instruments were concluded. Thus, the provisions of the Helsinki Final Act may prove to be quite important in giving meaning to subsequent developments.

What has been said thus far concerning the relationship between the Final Act and the International Covenants cannot automatically be applied to the relationship between the Final Act and the European Convention on Human Rights. The right to receive information, as proclaimed in Article 10 of the European Convention, is based on the common understanding of the European states mentioned in the preamble of that treaty. This understanding is far more advanced, in a libertarian sense, than that which prevails on the universal plane. Generally speaking, it would not serve the object and purpose of the European Convention to interpret Article 10 on the basis of an instrument such as the Final Act, which clearly reflects the lack of a substantive consensus between East and West on the meaning of human rights.

THE ESCAPE CLAUSES IN THE FINAL ACT AND THE HUMAN RIGHTS INSTRUMENTS

The Final Act may also have a considerable impact on the escape clauses of the International Covenants. It is well known that the Eastern countries use as general principles the clauses that permit restrictions on the rights guaranteed by the International Covenants. This interpretation subjects all the rights to the limitations imposed under the national laws of Eastern countries.[12] From a purely juridical point of view, there is one argument against that practice: it is impermissible that an escape clause, which is clearly intended as an exception, be transformed into a general rule, thus, in effect, nullifying the grant of the fundamental right itself. But it must be admitted that this argument is not easy to apply in concrete cases, where one has to accept some necessity for limiting a given right.

Here again, the Final Act can be helpful in showing that restrictive clauses may not be used to disguise policies opposed to human rights in general and to the rights proclaimed in the Final Act and the International Covenants in particular. Of course, the Final Act also recognizes the right of the participating states to choose their political, social, economic, and cultural systems and their right to determine their laws and regulations. Undoubtedly, Eastern states will rely heavily on this inherent characteristic of sovereignty.[13]

But the Final Act has made it much more difficult to deny that a national legal system should be guided by a general respect for human rights. The rights mentioned expressly in guiding Principle VII are not tied to restrictive clauses. The reference to the International Covenants on Human Rights in the last paragraph of Principle VII cannot be used as a general reference to all escape clauses in the International Covenants, although this was the aim of some proposals.[14] That conclusion is clearly shown by the priority accorded the Universal Declaration of Human Rights, as well as the systematic structure of Principle VII as a whole. The reference to the International Covenants is not tied to the guarantee of any of the specific fundamental rights proclaimed in the first part of Principle VII, and the reference is framed in a clearly positive way. It cannot, therefore, be used to get out from under the human rights obligations that have been assumed.[15]

Of course, Basket III refers in many instances to national laws and practice. But here again, the provision clearly presupposes application in the spirit of the Final Act. It would appear that the very lack of a juridical character enables the Final Act to express more clearly the general humanitarian purpose underlying the whole instrument. The fact that certain specific subjects are addressed in Basket III makes it impossible to argue that these subjects may be regulated by national legislation without regard to the purpose of the Final Act.

Let us briefly provide some examples. Article 12 of the International Covenant on Civil and Political Rights establishes the right to travel: paragraph 1 guarantees freedom of movement within a country; paragraph 2 guarantees the right to leave any country, including the home country; and paragraph 3 acknowledges that these rights may be restricted by legislation. Those socialist states that do not recognize a general right to leave one's country interpret the restrictive clause as giving the state very broad legislative freedom. Here the chapter on Human Contacts in the Final Act may be relevant. It provides that family contacts, travel for personal as well as professional reasons, tourism, and meetings among young people shall all be facilitated. That provision shows that the participating states regard it as important, for humanitarian reasons, that no state be permitted to keep its citizens in complete isolation. Interpretations of Article 12 of the International Covenant should take into account this clear and detailed expression of what constitutes a humanitarian goal as to freedom of movement. Thus, the right to freedom of movement proclaimed in Article 12 of the International Covenant on Civil and Political Rights cannot be transformed into the opposite of this right by subjecting it to various general restrictions.

A similar situation exists with regard to the freedom of information in Article 19 of the International Covenant on Civil and Political Rights. Once again, the restrictions possible under paragraph 3 may be used to deprive the right to information of its meaning in a number of very important respects. A state which forbids the sale of foreign newspapers for reasons of national security or public order could argue that it was acting in accordance with the covenant, interpreting paragraph 3 literally.[16] Of course, that result cannot be accepted under the covenant, although the public order exception is indeed very broad. The literal interpretation is even more clearly unacceptable if one takes the Final Act into account. Eastern and Western countries have agreed, in the section on information in the Final Act, that the dissemination of newspapers and printed publications from other participating states shall be facilitated. That agreement makes it invalid to contend that the distribution of foreign newspapers is generally dangerous to national security and public order. Reference to the Final Act, then, makes it clear that the right to seek information under Article 19 of the covenant cannot be restricted so as to completely exclude all foreign newspapers.

As these examples show, the Final Act may influence the interpretation of the escape clauses of the International Covenants in two distinct yet interrelated ways. First, the relationship between a given right and restrictive clause has been clarified by the understanding reached in the Final Act. Second, the Final Act may be used to interpret the limits on restrictions considered to be necessary. If the states have clearly expressed their agreement in the Final Act to cooperate on a specific subject, they may not urge, under the covenants, that it is necessary completely to restrict the human rights within that same subject. To guarantee the freedoms in the International Covenants, one must know how to interpret restrictive clauses. Clearly, therefore, the effect of the Final Act on the escape clauses of the International Covenants deserves further attention. It may well be that the legal impact of the Final Act on the human rights field will be felt quite significantly in this area.

In this connection, the European Convention on Human Rights and its restrictive clauses should also be mentioned. As a matter of general interpretation, as previously noted, the Final Act could hardly be used to interpret an instrument which has been concluded by a group of states with a much clearer common understanding of the human rights included in the treaty. However, concerning the problem of restrictive clauses, the understanding reached at Helsinki might at least indicate what restrictions are impermissible also on the European level. It is much less likely that the Final Act's interpretation of restrictions will be of greater importance on the European level than on the universal level, although its theoretical relevance cannot be excluded. Clearly, however, under the European Convention, the public order escape clauses and similar restrictions can never be invoked to lower a standard accepted in the Final Act.[17]

THE PROBLEM OF REMEDIES IN THE FINAL ACT AND IN THE INTERNATIONAL COVENANTS

Both U.N. covenants contain provisions establishing a system, albeit quite weak, to supervise their implementation. The Final Act does not set up any institution to guarantee the implementation of its provisions. The follow-up chapter of the Final Act makes it clear, however, that implementation shall be a matter for discussion at the forthcoming meetings. It is, therefore, appropriate to explore the relationship between the clearly underdeveloped system of remedies provided for in the International Covenants and in the Final Act.

The International Covenant on Economic, Social, and Cultural Rights provides for a reporting system (Part IV). The U.N. Commission on Human Rights may, under that system, make general recommendations on the information it receives.[18] The International Covenant on Civil and Political Rights does not go much further. Again, the states must submit reports. The committee set up under the covenant must study those reports and may submit general comments to the state concerned. Only if a state has recognized the procedure under Article 41 may the committee receive a complaint by a state that another party has violated the covenant. But even then, the committee's powers are limited to offering its good offices.[19] The committee lacks the power to find that the covenant has been violated, which is a feature clearly distinguishing this procedure from that of the European Convention on Human Rights. Only under the Optional Protocol may the committee forward "its views" (including its views as to the possible violation of the covenant) to the states and individuals concerned.

The system of remedies to be found in the covenants is obviously inadequate. This is hardly surprising because state interests are very much at stake in these matters. What seems more dangerous, however, than the mere absence of efficient remedies is the possible consequence of these provisions on the right of states *inter se* to take up the matter of the implementation of the International Covenants in the context of the states' other bilateral or multilateral relations.

Neither covenant answers the question of how exclusive its system of supervision is intended to be. Article 23 of the International Covenant on Economic, Social, and Cultural Rights provides that international action to implement an enunciated right may include conventions, the adoption of recommendations, and meetings. It does not mention that states may act bilaterally.

The International Covenant on Civil and Political Rights expressly states in Article 44 that its implementation provisions shall apply without prejudice to the procedures prescribed in the field of human rights by or under the constituent instruments and the conventions of the U.N. and of the specialized agencies. This means that the rules developed in the U.N. Commission on Human Rights to deal with situations that reveal a "consistent pattern of gross violations of human rights" have not been abrogated by the new procedure.[20] Article 44 adds the important clarification that its provisions shall not prevent the state parties from having recourse to other procedures for settling a dispute, in accordance with general or special international agreements in force between them. It is noteworthy that Article 62 of the European Convention on Human Rights contains an express waiver by the contracting parties of their right to use other means of settlement than those provided for in the convention.[21] The clarification in Article 44 of the International Covenant on Civil and Political Rights is of considerable importance. It shows, primarily, that states may have recourse to the normal procedures, including the ones mentioned in Article 33 of the U.N. Charter. But these procedures require that the states invoke a right violated by the other party. This procedure may not be possible under the covenants when no national of the state taking up the matter is involved.[22] The obiter dictum of the International Court of Justice in the *Barcelona Traction* case, concerning the protection of human rights, may be significant here. Although the Court recognized that basic human rights create obligations *erga omnes,* it emphasized later on that, on the universal level, "instruments which embody human rights do not confer on States the capacity to protect the victims of infringements of such rights irrespective of their nationality." Although the International Covenants had not yet entered into force at the time this judgment was delivered, it is difficult to believe that the Court did not also consider them.[23]

A formal démarche accusing another state of a breach of the International Covenants may easily be answered with the argument that the existing procedures laid down in the International Covenants should be used to settle the matter. Indeed, the International Covenant on Civil and Political Rights provides for a formal communication to bring the matter of a breach to the attention of another state party [Article 41(a)]. But Article 41(a) applies only if the states concerned have first recognized the complaint procedure envisaged under Article 41. It may be argued, on the other hand, that, without specific rules to the contrary, a party to a multilateral treaty always has the right to complain to the other parties about their failure to implement the treaty. In general, this right must certainly be recognized.[24] But it is very difficult to find practice confirming this right in situations in which specific complaint procedures have been set up.[25] In such cases states are more likely to avoid asserting a formal right and will instead address the other party less formally. Although the difference between these two approaches may not be great, it must be discussed to explain the impact of the Final Act on the problem of redress.

By facilitating the discussion of human rights issues, the Final Act may prove to be of considerable importance in the area of implementation. In the Final Act, the participating states stated their determination to respect human rights in their mutual relations. They undertook, jointly and separately, to try to promote universal and effective respect for human rights. Furthermore, they declared their resolve to implement the provisions of the Final Act, unilaterally or bilaterally, by negotiations with the other participating states. In defining human rights, the Final Act expressly mentions the U.N. Charter, the Universal Declaration, and the International Covenants. The signatory states of the Final Act manifestly recognized that, for them, respect for human rights is an international concern. Their failure to set up any institutional framework makes it possible for them to discuss human rights issues bilaterally or multilaterally. Of course, the Final Act creates no rights or obligations under international law. These states have, however, come to an informal agreement about their common interest in the field of human rights. It may, therefore, be much more efficient for them to take up the matter of human rights on that basis, rather than to use the formal procedures of the International Covenants. In the final analysis, the more subtle system of Helsinki may prove to be the strong one.

NOTES

1. Case concerning the Barcelona Traction, Light and Power Company, Limited, [1970] I.C.J. paras. 34, 32.

2. The International Convention on the Elimination of All Forms of Racial Discrimination was certainly another instrument alluded to by the Court, since protection from racial discrimination was expressly mentioned in the judgment's first statement concerning human rights. (*Id.,* paras. 24, 32.)

3. *Id.,* paras. 91, 47.

4. *Compare* principle X of the Declaration on Guiding Principles as well as the statement that the Final Act is not eligible for registration under Article 102 of the U.N. Charter. Russell, *The Helsinki Declaration: Brobdingnag or Lilliput?* 70 AM. J. INT'L L. 242, at 246, ff. (1976).

5. The problem concerning the Final Act is discussed at length by Schweisfurth, *Zur Frage der Rechtsnatur, Verbindlichkeit und völkerrechtlichen Relevanz der KSZE-Schlussakte,* 36 ZEITSCHRIFT FÜR AUSLÄNDISCHES ÖFFENTLICHES RECHT UND VÖLKERRECHT, 681 ff. (1976).

6. Frowein, *Der Beitrag der internationalen Organisationen zur Entwicklung des Völkerrechts,* 37 ZEITSCHRIFT FÜR AUSLÄNDISCHES ÖFFENTLICHES RECHT UND VÖLKERRECHT, 147 ff. (1976).

7. *Compare* Chapter 4 in this volume.

8. *See* Chapter 3 in this volume.

9. The legal character of the Final Act is also discussed by Skubiszewski, Delbrück and Rotfeld *in* DRITTES DUETSCH-POLNISCHES JURISTEN-KOLLOQUIUM, VOL. I, KSZE-SCHLUSSAKTE (R. Bernhardt, J. von Münch, W. Rudolf, eds. 1977), Völkerrecht und Aussenpolitik.

10. VERDROSS-SIMMA, UNIVERSELLES VÖLKERRECHT, 599 ff. (1976).

11. It is well known that the freedom to receive foreign newspapers is severely restricted in many Eastern countries. For factual information see Rudolf, *Zusammenarbeit in humanitären und anderen Bereichen gemäss der KSZE-Schlussakte,* DRITTES DEUTSCH-POLNISCHES JURISTEN-KOLLOQUIUM, above, note 9, at 97, 119 ff; Chapter 7 in this volume.

12. *Compare* Russell, above, note 4, at 268 ff.

13. The Polish author Z. Kędzia stresses the reference to sovereign equality when discussing the human rights provisions of the Final Act, DRITTES DEUTSCH-POLNISCHES JURISTEN-KOLLOQUIUM, above, note 9, at 71, 73 ff.

14. Russell, above, note 4, at 268 ff.

15. Rudolf, above, note 11, at 108.

16. Concerning this problem, *see* above, note 11.

17. The European Court of Human Rights has tried to address the problem of whether a restriction is necessary in the *Handyside Judgment* of December 7, 1976.

18. See Schwelb, *Entry into Force of the International Covenants on Human Rights and the Optional Protocol to the International Covenant on Civil and Political Rights,* 70 AM. J. INT'L L., 516 (1976).

19. For a detailed discussion see Schwelb, *Civil and Political Rights: The International Measures of Implementation,* 62 AM. J. INT'L L. 827 (1968).

20. Schwelb, above, note 18, at 515, notes that a review of the ECOSOC procedure may be necessary under the specific resolutions.

21. The question of how far the parties may take up the matter bilaterally is left open.

22. Egon Schwelb, certainly one of those best qualified to judge the history of the International Covenants, points out that the procedure under Article 41 of the International Covenant on Civil Rights is a sort of *actio popularis,* in which the complaining state does not necessarily assert its own rights (above, note 19, at 847 ff). That is, indeed, the

prevailing view for the procedure under Article 24 of the European Convention of Human Rights (*see* European Commission of Human Rights, *Austria v. Italy,* 4 Y. B. EUROPEAN CONVENTION OF HUMAN RIGHTS 140). By bringing the complaint, the state is upholding the public order of Europe.

23. *See* above, note 3.

24. B. SIMMA, DAS REZIPROZITÄTSELEMENT IM ZUSTANDEKOMMEN VÖLKERRECHTLICHER VERTRÄGE, 190 (1972); whether a state party to a multilateral treaty not specially affected by a breach may use reprisals or terminate the treaty is much more doubtful. Article 60 of the Vienna Convention on the Law of Treaties limits the right to terminate the treaty in such a case to a party specially affected [Article 60(2)(b)] or to a treaty of such character that a material breach of its provisions radically changes the position of every party with respect to the further performance of its obligations [Article 60(2)(c)]. A very good discussion of the extremely difficult background of Article 60 and the problem discussed here may be found in Simma, *Reflections on Art. 60 of the Vienna Convention on the Law of Treaties and its Background in General International Law,* 20 ÖSTERREICHISCHE ZEITSCHRIFT FÜR ÖFFENTLICHES RECHT, 5, at 45 ff., 67 ff. (1970).

25. Humphrey, *The International Law of Human Rights in the Middle Twentieth Century,* THE PRESENT STATE OF INTERNATIONAL LAW AND OTHER ESSAYS (M. Bos, ed. 1973) 75, at 86, seems to interpret the procedure under Article 41 of the International Covenant on Civil and Political Rights as being exclusive. Capotorti, *The International Measures of Implementation Included in the Covenants on Human Rights,* INTERNATIONAL PROTECTION OF HUMAN RIGHTS (A. Eide and A. Schou, eds. 1968) 131, treats only the procedure laid down in the International Covenants. For an earlier discussion, *see* Golsong, *Implementation of International Protection of Human Rights,* 110 RECUEIL DES COURS, 1 ff. (1963 III).

6 The Helsinki Declaration and Self-Determination

by ANTONIO CASSESE

It has been held that the Helsinki Declaration does not propound new ideas on the question of self-determination of peoples but merely reaffirms current U.N. doctrine on the matter. This view, which might seem correct at first glance, is in my opinion decidedly questionable. To disprove it and to put the Helsinki Declaration into the right perspective, it is necessary to survey briefly how the principle of self-determination has evolved on a universal level, i.e., within the framework of the United Nations. It should then be possible to pinpoint the important innovations of the Helsinki Declaration.

THE PROCLAMATION OF SELF-DETERMINATION AT A UNIVERSAL LEVEL

The U.N. Charter

The formulation adopted in Articles 1 and 55 of the U.N. Charter considers self-determination only as a goal, a political policy of the organization and its members, but not as a definite obligation to be fulfilled immediately. This formulation was the result of a compromise between the Soviet Union, resolutely anticolonialist (the statements made by Molotov in 1945 testify to this),[1] and the colonialist countries, in particular France, Belgium, and Great Britain (in 1943 Churchill stated that the principle of self-determination upheld by the Atlantic Charter did not apply to the colonies, but only aimed at restoring the sovereignty and self-government of the European states and nations that had been under the Nazi yoke).[2]

What specific content did the authors of the U.N. Charter want to give to the principle of self-determination? Three characteristics can be inferred from the normative context in which the principle appears or from the preparatory work.

In the first place, self-determination was considered only as a means of furthering the development of friendly relations among states and to strengthen universal peace. It was regarded, not as an independent value, but only as secondary to the goal of peace, with the obvious consequence that it might and indeed should be set aside when its fulfillment would give rise to tension and conflict among states.

Secondly, the principle of self-determination was accepted only insofar as it implied the right to self-government of peoples and not the right of secession.[3] Thus, as long ago as 1945, the territorial integrity of states—which, as we shall see shortly, has acquired enormous importance in recent years—was held to be paramount. At that time, however, their need clearly had a conservative connotation in that it included, among other things, the safeguarding of colonial empires. Furthermore, it meant the reversal of Wilson's approach to self-determination; immediately after World War I he had invoked the principle of self-determination to divide and separate pre-existent states to give birth to new states based on national ties.

Thirdly, it was specified that "self-determination" was to mean real and genuine choice. It is worth remembering—since it is usually overlooked—that, in 1945, the following was agreed to in San Francisco: "an essential element of the principle in question is a free and genuine expression of the will of the people, which avoids cases of the alleged expression of the popular will, such as those used for their own ends by Germany and Italy in later (sic) years".[4] This reference to Italy and Germany throws a lot of light on the question: it shows that forms of totalitarian oppression, even though dressed up in legalitarian trappings, were to be considered a denial of self-determination of peoples.[5]

In short, it can be said that the U.N. Charter neither defines self-determination (considering it more or less synonymous with "self-government") nor distinguishes between "external" and "internal" self-determination. Nonetheless, certain elements of the U.N. Charter had considerable vitality (for example, the concept of self-determination as an effective and genuine choice and, in particular, as an antitotalitarian choice) and were destined, in the course of time, to bear fruit.

The Divergence Between the Socialist and the Western Doctrine of Self-Determination

The development of the principle of self-determination set out in the U.N. Charter was unforeseen. The original promise of the U.N. Charter was upset both by normative innovation and by events. The anticolonialist force of the principle spread while its other possible meanings grew progressively less important. These developments resulted from the predominance of the socialist doctrine of self-determination over the doctrine of the Western world and from the impetus gained by the anticolonialist movement during the postwar period (the Bandung Conference was held in 1955). The essential points of the two conceptions will be briefly examined.

Socialist countries understand self-determination essentially as the liberation of non-self-governing peoples from colonial domination.[6] They have broadened the concept—under pressure from African and Arab countries—to include liberation from racist domination (South Africa and Southern Rhodesia) and from foreign occupation (Arab territories occupied by Israel). Moreover, with the support of Afro-Asian countries (which worry that the collapse of colonialism might lead to the breaking up of the former colonial territories), the socialist countries deny that self-determination can legitimate secessions. Thus, to these theorists, self-determination means only "external" self-determination and only applies to peoples subject to colonial or racist rule or to foreign occupation. The achievement of independent status by peoples living in nonracist, sovereign states entails the implementation of self-determination. This applies in particular to socialist states: "only in socialist States and through the sovereignty achieved by them can self-determination be completely realized".[7] In particular, for sovereign and independent states, self-determination becomes tantamount to the right to nonintervention. This point is very important and deserves particular stress. According to the socialist countries, self-determination, considered as the right to nonintervention, means the right that foreign states shall not interfere in the life of the community *against the will of the government*. It does not mean that a foreign state shall not interfere in the life of the community against the interests of the population, but that it may only do so at the request or at least with the tacit approval of the government.

Western countries have, on many occasions, attacked this outlook for being too restrictive and onesided. They maintain that the rights of peoples oppressed by totalitarian regimes must be recognized and that in any case self-determination must include respect for fundamental freedoms and the basic rights of individuals. The close link between self-determination and individual human rights is one of the main features of the Western doctrine. As the U.S. delegate to the Third Committee of the General Assembly put it in 1972:

> Freedom of choice is indispensable to the exercise of the right of self-determination. For this freedom of choice to be meaningful, there must be corresponding freedom of thought, conscience, expression, movement and association. Self-determination entails legitimate, lively dissent and testing at the ballot box with frequent regularity.[8]

Another distinguishing trait of the Western view is its emphasis on the universality of the principle of self-determination. According to Western states, the principle at issue must be regarded as applying to all peoples, not just to certain specific categories of peoples. This conception is substantially right, though it contains a basic flaw. It has often been used to oppose or at least to curb the socialist countries' anticolonial drive, to defend the interests of the colonial powers. The Western countries have had difficulty understanding that, in the period from about 1945 to 1965, it was necessary for the concept of self-determination to be identified with that of anticolonialism because, at that time, the end of colonial dominion was the principal aim in the struggle for human freedom.

Normative Developments Of The U.N. Charter: The 1966 Covenants On Human Rights

These two doctrines of self-determination could not easily be reconciled. Indeed, one of them—the Western conception—gradually lost ground and was, to a great extent, superseded by the other, although Western countries managed to slow down the realization of self-determination by colonial and other dependent territories. The clash between the two doctrines was also apparent in the "normative" texts which were drafted on the matter by the U.N., and in which the basic differences were to some extent papered over; the socialist view ultimately prevailed.

While space does not permit examination of all the U.N. resolutions that touch upon the point, the two Covenants on Human Rights adopted by the General Assembly in 1966 should be examined in some detail.

The first articles of both covenants—which refer to self-determination in identical terms—have two relevant features.[9] First, they clarify an important aspect of the relationship between the concepts of individual human rights and the self-determination of peoples. Some learned authors have argued that the communal right of self-determination and the rights of individuals are not comparable concepts and, therefore, ought not to be included in the same package.[10] In fact, the inclusion of the right of self-determination in the covenants was intended to emphasize what should by now be self-evident: that there is little sense in recognizing the rights and freedoms of individuals if the community in which the individuals live is not free. The right of self-determination is an essential precondition for the effective realization of individual rights and freedoms.

Another important feature of the first articles is that they sanction both internal and external self-determination. With regard to the former, all contracting states agreed to recognize the right to self-determination of peoples living under territorial jurisdiction of the states. External self-determination is applicable to non-self-governing territories and trust territories: contracting states responsible for such territories undertook to recognize their right to self-determination. Thus the socialist and Afro-Asian view, that external self-determination applies only to colonial situations, is codified in the covenants.

These characteristics, together with the fact that the covenants are the only international agreements in force which explicitly make it the duty of states to grant self-determination, might lead to an overestimation of the importance of the covenants. They have, however, their limits. In particular, they are marred by compromise and ambiguity. Thus, the definition of self-determination given in Article 1, paragraph 1, of each is vague and all-embracing. ("All peoples have the right to self-determination. By virtue of that right they freely determine their political status and freely pursue their economic, social and cultural development.") From the context in which it appears, this norm certainly refers to internal self-determination. However, the reference is neither clear nor satisfactory. For example, what does it mean to say that people, let us say the Italian or the French people, have the right to "freely determine their political status" (internally)? Does it mean self-government, or freedom to choose a democratic representative government? Undoubtedly, the formulation of the covenants is evasive. Furthermore, the third paragraph of Article 1, in attempting to specify the nature of the contracting states' obligation to grant self-determination, uses a very general wording: "The States Parties to the present Covenant. . .shall promote the realization of the right of self-determination." The same provision adds a reference to the U.N. Charter which helps to confuse the issue further: "The States Parties to the present Covenant . . . shall respect that . . . right, in conformity with the provisions of the Charter of the United Nations." What this reference to the Charter is meant to signify remains a mystery. Obviously it is one of those pleasant-sounding clauses which, by their very vagueness, tend to make the implementation of the right sanctioned by the norm difficult and problematical. The only thing that can be said with some degree of certainty is that the reference is intended to exclude the right of secession.

To conclude: the covenants, though relatively specific as regards external self-determination (where, however, only the socialist and Afro-Asian outlook is reflected), are reticent and evasive about internal self-determination.

The Declaration on Friendly Relations (1970)

The next and—for the time being—last U.N. pronouncement which upholds the right of self-determination is the Declaration on Friendly Relations and Cooperation among States adopted by consensus, in 1970, by the General Assembly. Its chief merit is that it collects and endeavors to clarify (insofar as is possible for a U.N. document) previous resolutions on the subject adopted by the world organization. As far as self-determination is concerned, however, the Declaration suffers from the same defects of ambiguity and vagueness that marred the covenants. Moreover, these defects are compounded, because the Declaration makes an attempt to cover all issues relating to this complex matter.

The Western countries spared no efforts to affirm their thesis that the principle of self-determination must be considered universal in nature. And the first paragraph of the Principle seems to uphold their views. It states:

> By virtue of the principle of equal rights and self-determination of peoples enshrined in the Charter of the United Nations, all peoples have the right freely to determine, without external interference, their political status and to pursue their economic, social and cultural development, and every State has the duty to respect this right in accordance with the provisions of the Charter.

The reference to "all peoples" and the unqualified content of this paragraph have led a few Western authors, who took part in the drafting of the Declaration on Friendly Relations, to contend that it upholds the doctrine of the universality of self-determination.[11] This interpretation does not reflect the actual purport of the Declaration accurately. For one thing, the wording of the quoted paragraph is so sweeping and indefinite that, like Article 1 of the covenants, it does not offer any concrete indication as to what is really meant by self-determination. The concept of self-determination laid down in this provision is so general that a socialist state or a socialist scholar could easily argue it indicates only the right of the peoples living in sovereign states to be free from external interference and is thus nothing other than the right of the *state* to nonintervention in its domestic affairs.

Second, and more important, the subsequent paragraphs qualify the general and all-embracing definition set forth in the first paragraph. They ultimately restrict it in such a way as to make it arguable that the Declaration on Friendly Relations substantially upholds the gist of the socialist and Afro-Asian view of the meaning of self-determination. It is apparent from the Declaration that external self-determination can be identified essentially as the liberation of peoples from colonial rule and from "alien subjugation, domination and exploitation".[12] According to the 1970 Declaration, this can be brought about through the "establishment of a sovereign and independent State, the free association or integration with an independent State or the emergence into any other political status freely determined by a people." The peoples who have the right to this form of self-determination also have the right to use force to obtain self-determination (when force is used to deny it) and the right to seek and receive outside support in the struggle for national liberation. A significant novelty of the Declaration concerns internal self-determination, i.e., extending the right to a people or a minority group living in an independent and sovereign state. For the first time in the history of the U.N., the conditions and limits of this category of self-determination are specified.[13] Internal self-determination is realized when the state has a "government representing the whole people belonging to the territory without distinction as to race, creed or colour." When these conditions are lacking, the people or the minority can demand that their right of self-determination be respected and, in pursuit of the exercise of that right, they are even entitled to secede.

The aspect of the Declaration on Friendly Relations that is most open to criticism is the position it takes on internal self-determination. In practice, the right of self-determination is only recognized for peoples living under racist regimes such as those of South Africa or Southern Rhodesia. In stating that self-determination cannot be invoked when (1) there is a representative government and (2) in particular, this government represents the whole people without distinction as to race, creed, or color, the Declaration specifies two conditions that are clearly lacking in only a few limited cases. Nobody can say with certainty if and when a government is representative under the 1970 Declaration. ("Representative" according to the criteria of Western parliamentary democracies or of socialist political systems? And can one say that an authoritarian government is representative if, though not regularly elected nor based on consensus of opinion, it is nonetheless formed so as to reflect all the more important segments of the population?). In actual fact, the Declaration leaves it to governments themselves to decide whether or not they are representative (aside from the exceptional cases, such as South Africa or Southern Rhodesia, where it is unanimously accepted that the governments are not representative and discriminate on the basis of race and color). No reference is made in the Declaration to political, economic, and social oppression. Thus, over the years, the reference made in San Francisco in 1945 to the need for self-determination for peoples living under oppressive and totalitarian regimes has been lost. The need to safeguard national unity and territorial integrity has, in effect, overridden the demand for wide and effective recognition of the right of self-determination.

Yet another drawback of the Declaration on Friendly Relations is that it reverts to the viewpoint of the U.N. Charter (which may have been justified in 1945 in view of the recent conflicts and the limited awareness of the principle of self-determination), that self-determination is a means for promoting friendly relations among states. As previously pointed out, if the principle is considered in this way, there is a risk that the principle of self-determination will be forgotten whenever its implementation may involve tension and conflict among states. As this usually does occur, this view of the concept conceals an element of danger which may lead to the substantial annihilation of the right to self-determination.

Finally, the question of the legal standing of the principle of self-determination as proclaimed in the Declaration on Friendly Relations remains. Can it be argued that this principle has turned into a rule of general international law? Indisputably, the Declaration as such is not a legally binding text. On some points, however, it restates and clarifies international law, while on others it accelerates the law-making process. So far as self-determination is concerned the vagueness and ambiguity of the Declaration, which stem from and are evidence of substantial differences of opinion, could not warrant the view that all the provisions of the Declaration codify existing norms of international law. Nor could it be held that the principle as embodied in the Declaration has become binding international law simply because the Declaration was adopted by consensus by practically all states that are members of the international community; this consensus was achieved precisely because the Declaration was not regarded as imposing legal duties. The Declaration has contributed to the formation of a set of general rules concerning the principle of self-determination, but not all of its provisions have become customary law. Only those on which a broad measure of substantial and unreserved agreement was possible have evolved into international rules. These provisions are the following:

1. Peoples under colonial or alien domination have a right to external self-determination, i.e., to attain the status of sovereign and independent states or any other international political status freely determined by the peoples themselves.

2. Peoples under racist regimes have the right to internal and external self-determination, i.e., either to free themselves from their regimes by achieving self-government or to secede from the racist state.

3. States controlling peoples who find themselves in one of the aforementioned situations have a duty to respect and implement this right and in particular to refrain from using force to deprive peoples of their right to self-determination.

4. Third-party States are, on the one hand, duty-bound to refrain from interfering with the exercise of this right and, on the other hand, authorized to grant peoples struggling for their self-determination any form of support (short of the dispatch of troops).

Of course, these rules have acquired the status of law not merely because of their proclamation in the Declaration on Friendly Relations, but because they had already been set forth to a great extent in several U.N. resolutions and—what is more important—they had already been acted upon by a large majority of member states before the adoption of the Declaration. Furthermore, these rules have been restated and implemented by a great many states since 1970. They have *inter alia* been incorporated in legal instruments. It suffices to mention here Article 1 of the First Additional Protocol to the 1949 Geneva Conventions on the Victims of War, which was agreed upon in 1974 and formally adopted by the Geneva Conference in 1977. This article regards armed conflicts where "peoples are fighting against colonial domination or alien occupation and against racist regimes" as wars fought in the exercise of the right of self-determination, "as enshrined in the Charter of the United Nations and the Declaration" on Friendly Relations. The importance of this provision should not be underestimated; in a way, it gives authentication to the principle of self-determination set forth in the 1970 Declaration on Friendly Relations.

The Value of U.N. Actions on Self-Determination

Nobody can deny that, from many points of view, U.N. activity has been very praiseworthy. First, the principle of self-determination has been codified, and its inherent implications have been developed with regard to anti-colonialism and similar situations (racist regimes, foreign occupation). In short, the general and embryonic concept adopted in the U.N. Charter has become articulate and forceful. However, it is more important that the work of clarification and definition has been accompanied by concrete action aimed at implementing the principle and that this action has achieved considerable results. The movement towards anticolonialism (in the widest sense of the term) has been coupled with anxiety lest self-determination should prejudice the territorial integrity of non-self-governing peoples.

The work of the U.N. has, however, been onesided in that—in line with socialist and Afro-Asian doctrines—it has concentrated primarily on external self-determination of certain categories of peoples and has tended to neglect internal self-determination. This may seem to some extent justified in a period (1945-1965) in which anticolonialism and other allied movements played such an important part; but it is perhaps less so now that almost all non-self-governing peoples have acquired their independence. The U.N. has continued to defend with tenacity the stronghold of state sovereignty and territorial integrity; although unquestionably important, these values are protected by other norms and do not require that the principle of self-determination be interpreted as the right to noninterference by foreign states. The principles governing internal self-determination laid down by the U.N. are decidedly moderate and cautious and reflect a definite tendency to defend established governments even when this is detrimental to the effective implementation of the rights of peoples.

THE HELSINKI DECLARATION

Introduction

Turning now to Europe, it is obvious that none of the three situations relating to external self-determination referred to in many U.N. documents exists there. The only colonial situation is Gibraltar, a very controversial and unclear issue that, because of its anomalous character, the world organization has so far been unable to settle. There are no racist regimes in Europe comparable to those of South Africa or Southern Rhodesia; and, with the (relative) exception of Cyprus, no forms of alien occupation exist that can be equated with the Israeli occupation of Arab countries. The logical conclusion should be that, to a very great extent, the principle of external and internal self-determination has already been realized in Europe (as well as in the United States and Canada) and that, therefore, it would be pointless to codify and reaffirm it in some sort of regional European instrument. Yet, situations exist in Europe which come within the purview of a broader concept of self-determination than that embodied in the U.N. instruments. Reference can be made to the German nation, currently divided into two sovereign states, or to the Irish people, part of whom are now under British rule in Northern Ireland.[14] Even more serious is the problem of ethnic, national, or linguistic minorities living in a number of European countries. These minorities clearly raise a question of internal self-determination. The same problem, though in a different context, arises with regard to peoples living in European authoritarian states— provided, of course, a more comprehensive concept of internal self-determination is accepted than that reflected in U.N. texts.

The Federal Republic of Germany, one of the countries having a large stake in the issue of self-determination, urged the inclusion of a principle relating thereto in the Helsinki Declaration. The FRG's main purpose was to facilitate the possible future reunification of the two Germanys.[15] As was stated at Helsinki by the Foreign Minister of the FRG in 1973, ". . .it is the political aim of the Federal Republic of Germany to help create a state of peace in Europe in which the German nation can regain its unity in free self-determination."[16]

The Federal Republic of Germany was, therefore, primarily interested in proclaiming external self-determination. Following the West German move, a few states offered proposals covering the principle in question. The Soviet Union and France advanced formulations that followed traditional lines, though they were couched in such general terms that they were applicable even to peoples living in sovereign (nonracist) states. Two other countries, Yugoslavia and the Netherlands, proposed innovative and forward-looking formulas that covered situations remaining outside U.N. texts.

The Four Texts Proposed in 1973

The Soviet proposal stated that one of the "principles of primary significance" to be strictly respected and observed by states was that of equal rights and self-determination of peoples ". . .in accordance with which all peoples possess the right to establish the social regime and to choose the form of government which they consider expedient and necessary to secure the economic, social and cultural development of their country."[17]

It is apparent that this definition only referred to internal self-determination. It neither borrowed the U.N. formulations nor defined self-determination precisely. In particular, it did not specify whether self-determination is a right that is implemented merely by the establishment of a sovereign state or whether it is a permanent right of any people to political and social change. Furthermore, the Soviet text made no reference to the right of peoples to determine their status free from any outside interference.

The lacunae of the Soviet proposal were filled in by the French text, which was exhaustive, though it did not depart from traditional concepts and formulations. It read as follows:

> . . . En vertu de ce principe, tous les peuples ont le droit de déterminer leur statut politique *interne et externe en toute liberté et sans ingérence extérieure* et de poursuivre leur développement économique, social et culturel et tous les Etats ont le devoir de respecter ce droit. Les Etats participants considèrent que le respect de ces principes doit guider leurs relations mutuelles comme il doit caractériser les rapports entre tous les Etats.[18]

As previously pointed out, the next two proposals were really innovative. The text suggested by Yugoslavia read as follows:

> The participating States reaffirm the *universal significance* of the principle of equal rights and self-determination by peoples for the promotion of friendly relations and co-operation between States in Europe and the world as a whole and *for the eradication of any form of subjugation or of subordination contrary to the will of the peoples concerned.*

> They will observe the right of every people freely to determine its political status and to pursue, independently and without external interference, its political, economic, social and cultural development. They will refrain from any forcible or other action denying the equal rights or the right of self-determination of any people.[19]

This definition is very significant, not so much for its comprehensiveness (it encompasses both internal and external self-determination) but for two other reasons. First, it places considerable emphasis on the universality of the principle in question—namely, on a feature of the principle that thus far had been stressed only by Western countries. Secondly, the Yugoslav proposal is based on freedom from any form of (outside) interference. This is first made clear in the sentence referring to the "eradication of any form of subjugation or of subordination contrary to the will of the peoples concerned." As—except for the anomalous situation of Cyprus—no people in Europe find themselves in one of the situations referred to in U.N. instruments as "foreign occupation," reference is here made to other situations neglected in U.N. texts, such as alien economic, political, or military domination. This point is then reiterated where it is stated that all people should determine their political status "independently and without external interference" and again where it is stated that all states must refrain "from any forcible or other action" denying the right in question.

The Netherlands proposal contained other elements which made it extremely original and significant. It stated:

> Each participating State will act in its relations with any other participating State in conformity with the principle of equal rights and self-determination of peoples laid down in the United Nations Charter.
>
> The participating States recognize the inalienable right of the people of every State freely *to choose, to develop, to adapt or to change* its political, economic, social and cultural systems without interference in any form by any other State or *group of States* and with *due respect to human rights and fundamental freedoms.*[20]

This text is striking, first, in that reference is made only to the U.N. Charter and not to the subsequent developments as incorporated, for example, in the Declaration on Friendly Relations. Thus, the specifications and also the qualifications of the principle of self-determination embodied in the post-1945 instruments are set aside. Yet, the most innovative element in the Netherlands proposal is that, in confining itself to internal self-determination, it spells out the right of all people *to change* their political, economic, social, or cultural system free from external interferences (be they exercised by a single state or by a group of states). Thus, the principle of self-determination becomes a safeguard against any inside or outside attempt at imposing preservation of the status quo. This was forcefully stressed in 1973 by the Dutch foreign minister, who observed:

> It can happen that a nation, which at some moment in its history has adopted a certain political or social-economic system, may want to adjust this system to changed circumstances. If in such a situation the peoples' democratic rights to adapt its structures were interfered with, either from within or especially from outside, tensions can build up which might endanger peace and security. The future system of relations in Europe should be flexible enough to allow for changes to occur without necessarily upsetting the international situation.[21]

The same view was also expressed by the foreign minister of Ireland.

> The first essential condition for European security as a whole is that each State exercise fair and democratic government capable of peaceful change and evolution in response to the evolving will of the people. Responsible government must have regard to the interests and aspirations of all sections of the community so that all these sections, even if in some cases unenthusiastically at times, can freely give their consent to it. Wherever injustice exists, wherever the rights of individuals are not fully respected, wherever governments are inflexible in response to the popular will, there are sown not only the seeds of internal discord but also the seeds of tension and instability in Europe as a whole. This is a truth which each of our governments has to recognize if we are serious in the pursuit of a genuine and lasting *détente* on our continent.[22]

This doctrine of self-determination is in clear contrast with the socialist countries' view that so far as nonracist sovereign states are concerned, internal self-determination is not relevant because the right of self-determination ceases to apply when a people has attained sovereignty. In the Netherlands proposal, the right is permanent, and its exercise cannot consume it. Further, it should be noted that, in the Netherlands proposal, the right in question is tied up with respect for human rights in a very original way: the right to social, political, economic, and cultural change must be exercised with due respect for human rights and fundamental freedoms. Self-determination is, thereby, made a one-way course of action: change and adaptation can only go in one direction, towards the realization of greater respect for human rights.

It is thus apparent that the thrust of the Netherlands proposal was an attempt to allow the Eastern European countries to evolve gradually towards a more humane form of socialism, free from interference from the Soviet Union.

The Discussion on the Texts

It is not easy to follow the debate that developed on the four proposals outlined above, partly because there are no records of some stages of the discussion and partly because the self-determination issue was closely intertwined with other questions. However, the following observations can be made.

First, a number of states expressed misgivings about the disruptive impact that the principle of self-determination might have on the territorial integrity of states. Since many of the 35 participating states have national minorities, the fear was expressed that an unqualified proclamation of the right of self-determination might kindle separatist aspirations to the detriment of national unity. Consequently, many Eastern and Western states urged that a defense be set up against this danger. Thus, general agreement evolved on the need to exclude national minorities from the purview of self-determination: only peoples, not minorities, should be the beneficiaries of the right.

While agreement on this point was reached quickly among most states, Western or Eastern, on other issues the two blocs appeared to be in sharp conflict. As far as external self-determination was concerned, the Soviet Union strongly opposed the Western action supporting the request of the Federal Republic of Germany that a clause be inserted providing, in general terms, for such situations as the reunification of the two Germanys. The U.S.S.R. tenaciously held to its thesis that external self-determination applies only to colonial-type situations.[23] A marked difference between Western and Eastern countries emerged also on internal self-determination. The former espoused the Dutch proposal, and thus tended to consider the principle the basis for gradual, peaceful, and democratic change, necessary for the adaptation to internal and international realities in conformity with the will of peoples. By contrast, the Soviet Union and some other socialist states vigorously upheld their view that, once a people has chosen a form of government or a certain social structure, its right to self-determination is to be regarded as implemented. It followed from the Soviet view that it did not make much sense to try to relate the principle of self-determination to peoples who, like those of the 35 countries, had already made a choice as to their internal political, social, economic, and cultural status. The Soviet Union, therefore, strongly opposed the verbs "adapt" and "change" contained in the Netherlands proposal, as well as the verb "choose." It also found unacceptable the word "inalienable" (right) that had been proposed by a number of Western delegations.

A different division emerged on another point. The Yugoslav proposal condemning "any form of subjugation or of subordination contrary to the will of the peoples concerned," while it received some support from Western countries, was firmly opposed by the Soviet Union and was eventually dropped. Apparently, that superpower feared the implications of the Yugoslav proposal within its satellite countries.

Another interesting point about the debates preceding the adoption of the Declaration on Guiding Principles in the Final Act is that some states, which, for domestic reasons, might have been expected to emphasize the principle of self-determination, refrained from doing so. Thus, both Spain and Ireland, while referring to the situations of Gibraltar and Northern Ireland respectively, did not explicitly connect them to the principle.[24] Nor was the principle referred to by Cyprus, Greece or Turkey when they mentioned the situation in Cyprus—a situation that clearly involves the right of self-determination.[25]

Principle VIII of the Helsinki Decalogue

Its Novelty.   The text eventually agreed upon reads as follows:

> The participating States will respect the equal rights of peoples and their right to self-determination, acting at all times in conformity with the purposes and principles of the Charter of the United Nations and with the relevant norms of international law, including those relating to territorial integrity of States.

By virtue of the principle of equal rights and self-determination of peoples, all peoples always have the right, in full freedom, to determine, when and as they wish, their internal and external political status, without external interference, and to pursue as they wish their political, economic, social and cultural development.

The participating States reaffirm the universal significance of respect for and effective exercise of equal rights and self-determination of peoples for the development of friendly relations among themselves as among all States; they also recall the importance of the elimination of any form of violation of this principle.

This formulation agreed upon at Helsinki apparently applies to both external and internal self-determination. To the extent to which it refers to internal self-determination, it substantially reflects the Western view and, in particular, the Netherlands proposal.

This being acknowledged, one can point out what may be considered the novelty, on the one hand, and the conservatism on the other hand, of the formulation adopted in 1975.

First, it must be stressed that the principle of self-determination applies to *all peoples,* regardless of whether they live in a sovereign and independent state. At first sight, this might seem to be a mere repetition of the first paragraph of the principle laid down in the Declaration on Friendly Relations. If it were so, the Helsinki Declaration would mark no improvement on U.N. instruments. The contrary is true, for the following reasons. The mention of "all peoples," when referring to peoples of sovereign states, is not devoid of practical consequences as it was in the case with the Declaration on Friendly Relations. In the Helsinki Declaration, the definition of self-determination that follows the reference to all peoples is not vague and all-embracing but specific and well-suited for application to the peoples of European states. Moreover, the word "always" ("all peoples always have the right") and the phrase "when and as they wish" ("have the right. . .to determine, when and as they wish, their internal and external political status") convey the idea that the right of self-determination is a *continuing* right, a right that continues to exist even after a people has chosen a certain form of government or a certain international status. Finally, the Helsinki Declaration has no clause (comparable to that included in the Declaration on Friendly Relations) that attempts to restrict the principle to sovereign states which have racist regimes. The absence of any such qualification bears out the view that, in the Helsinki Declaration, the principle of self-determination has a very wide range. Fourth, there is an extrinsic element confirming that the Helsinki Declaration applies primarily to peoples living in sovereign states. All the 35 states that participated in the European Conference are sovereign and independent states. They intended to set forth principles that would apply in their relations with one another. It follows that when, referring to self-determination of peoples, the participants intended to refer to their own people—that is, to people living in sovereign states. Consequently, the principle in the Helsinki Declaration addresses itself primarily, if not exclusively, to these people and not to people under colonial or foreign domination or under a racist regime.

The second significant feature of the Helsinki formulation is that it specifies by implication the scope of the word "peoples." Paragraph 4 of Principle VII ("Respect for human rights and fundamental freedoms, including the freedom of thought, conscience, religion or belief") states that

> [t]he participating States on whose territory national minorities exist will respect the right of persons belonging to such minorities to equality before the law, will afford them the full opportunity for the actual enjoyment of human rights and fundamental freedoms and will, in this manner, protect their legitimate interests in this sphere.

It does not follow that, simply because "national minorities" are dealt with in Principle VII, they are, therefore, not covered by Principle VIII. Theoretically, "national minorities" could be contemplated in both principles. If so, Principle VIII would give to minorities the right to self-determination; Principle VII would reserve to minorities individual rights with discriminatory treatment. However, a study of the debates preceding the adoption of Principle VIII makes it clear that there was complete agreement on the exclusion of "national minorities" (and *a fortiori* of religious, racial, or linguistic minorities) from the concept of "peoples." Principle VIII could only have been accepted if it would not disrupt the national and territorial unity of the 35 participants. Extending Principle VIII to "national minorities" would have given the minorities the right to external self-determination and hence the right to secede. Many of the signatory states are composed of different national groups; the governments of these states are naturally opposed to any international legitimizing of the centrifugal drive of those groups. Therefore, they could not have been expected to accept a liberal treatment of the phrase "national minorities," which treatment would do more than grant individual rights and fundamental freedoms to individuals who are members of the minority groups.[26] It would appear to be incontrovertible that the Helsinki Declaration, when it discusses the principle of self-determination, extends the right only to groups living in and identifying with sovereign states (for example, Italian, French, and Soviet citizens).

A third important feature of the principle as enunciated in the Helsinki Declaration is that it puts the relationship between the concepts of self-determination of human rights into the proper perspective. Paragraph 2 states ". . . all peoples always have the right, *in full freedom,* to determine . . . their internal and external political status, without external interference. . ." The phrase, "in full freedom," ought not to be interpreted as a mere positive expression of the negative phrase, "without external interference." It is a basic principle of interpretation that legal provisions should be construed so as to be "effective and useful" insofar as that is possible. One presumes that states avoid using superfluous expressions or words devoid of any practical meaning. To argue to the contrary, one must assume that the framers of the clause intentionally departed from this principle or, to put it more precisely, used a redundant expression to give a more forceful expression of their intent. A comparison with a parallel text, however, helps to refute this contention. Paragraph 1 of the Declaration on Friendly Relations states that "by virtue of the principle . . . all peoples have the right *freely* to determine, without external interference, their political status. . ." This wording is so weak and the adverb "freely" plays such a minor role that it is doubtful whether "freely" does not actually mean "free from external interference." The same conclusion cannot be drawn from the wording of the Helsinki Declaration, which is both stronger and clearer. Another and more conclusive argument can be advanced. It appears, both from the content of the provision and from the debates preceding the adoption of the Helsinki Declaration, that the phrase "in full freedom" reflects the Western view that the right of self-determination cannot be implemented if basic human rights and fundamental freedoms, in particular freedom of expression and association, are not ensured to all members of the people concerned. The philosophy behind this conception is that a people cannot make a real choice as to its political status or its economic, social, or cultural development when it is under an authoritarian government. The phrase, "in full freedom," is intended precisely to express this conception. It therefore sanctions the right of peoples to exercise self-determination free *from internal interference* (i.e., free from oppression by an authoritarian government). The expression "without external interference" denotes freedom *from possible encroachment by third states.*

To sum up, I believe that the Helsinki Declaration gives a definition of self-determination that breaks new ground in international relations. The originality of the definition does not concern external self-determination. In this respect, the Helsinki formulation stands out only for its comprehensiveness: it does not qualify and does provide for the choice of any kind of external political status. The innovative part of the Helsinki Declaration relates to internal self-determination. Here the wording agreed upon by the 35 states embodies the idea that self-determination means the permanent possibility for a people to choose a new social or political regime, to adapt the social or political structure to meet new demands. As the prime minister of the Netherlands observed at the Helsinki final session in 1975, and as set forth in the Declaration, the principle ". . . means that where the people express an opinion on their own destiny their voices shall be reflected in the policy of their governments."[27]

The conclusion is therefore warranted that the Helsinki Declaration emphasizes and delineates an approach to the concept of self-determination that had previously been conceived by the framers of the U.N. Charter (and that there is an antiauthoritarian, democratic thrust to the principle of self-determination), and that had all but disappeared from view in the post-1945 evolution of the United Nations. It is to the credit of the states gathered at the Conference on Security and Cooperation in Europe that they "revisited" the idea of self-determination, and in the process revitalized it.

The Traditional Facets of the Principle. As noted above, Principle VIII of the Decalogue does not introduce innovations on all issues relating to self-determination. It is traditional in at least two respects.

First, it recognizes that self-determination must not disrupt the territorial integrity of states. Paragraph 1 of the Principle provides that

> The participating states will respect the equal rights of peoples and their right to self-determination, acting at all times in conformity with the purposes and principles of the Charter of the United Nations and with the relevant norms of international law, including those relating to territorial integrity of states.

This would appear at first to be no more than a repetition of the well-known safeguard clause of the Declaration on Friendly Relations. On closer examination, however, the Helsinki text does show some originality. Respect for territorial integrity is a duty incumbent upon states, not on individuals or peoples. The reference to international rules concerning territorial integrity does not qualify the rights of people to self-determination; it only restricts the actions of states, which are duty-bound neither to support secessionist movements elsewhere nor to take any action likely to impair the territorial integrity of other states. It would follow that, under the Helsinki Declaration, a "people" can claim a right to secede if they consider secession the only means available to implement their right to self-determination (but keep in mind what was stressed above: "peoples" is not synonymous with "minorities;" the latter are not entitled to self-determination and certainly not to secession). By contrast, the safeguard clause of the Declaration on Friendly Relations is couched in terms that restrict the right to self-determination and oblige states not to interfere with the territorial integrity of nonracist sovereign states.

The rules on territorial integrity are mentioned in the Helsinki text as an example of the rules with which all states must comply in situations where a people is seeking to implement the right to self-determination. Other rules would be those prohibiting interference in the internal affairs of other states and forbidding the use of force. Indeed paragraph 1 of the Principle refers to the principles of the U.N. Charter and to the "relevant norms of international law," thus confirming and reinforcing that each principle must be interpreted in the light of the other principles contained in the Helsinki Declaration.

The second traditional aspect of the Helsinki principle is the reference it makes in paragraph 3 to the significance of self-determination "for the development of friendly relations" among states. In this, the Helsinki Declaration follows the U.N. Charter doctrine of self-determination as a means for achieving peaceful relations among states and not as a goal in itself. One might question if the authors of the Helsinki Declaration simply wished to pay respect to a "sacred" text, or whether they really intended to subordinate the realization of self-determination to the primary goal of the pursuit of friendly relations among states. Statements made by some delegations to the Helsinki Conference would seem to support the latter interpretation.[28]

THE RELATIONSHIP BETWEEN THE HELSINKI PRINCIPLE AND THE U.N. INSTRUMENTS AND CUSTOMARY INTERNATIONAL LAW

It would be difficult to disagree with the statement of the Secretary-General of the United Nations at the last session of the Conference, when he said that ". . . membership in the United Nations has surely provided *a common point of reference* in approaching many of the sensitive issues with which the conference has dealt."[29] Further, it is unarguable that the Helsinki Declaration was conceived as a means of reaffirming and reinforcing among the 35 participants the basic tenets of the U.N. Charter[30] by giving them a "new dimension in European space"[31] and "enhancing their implementation" among the participating states."[32] But it would not do justice to the significance of the Helsinki Declaration merely to say that it "is in line with the Charter of the U.N."[33] and that "it does not in any way conflict with or compete with" the principles of the U.N.[34] In fact, the Helsinki Declaration—while it does restate U.N. principles—in many respects goes further and also elaborates and refines those principles by adapting them to conditions obtaining in Europe. The remarks of the president of Finland, made at the conference in 1975, are pertinent in this regard:

> While it is based on the principles and purposes of the United Nations, the Declaration on Principles Guiding Relations between Participating States goes further than the Charter of the world organization, as it applies these principles to the particular conditions of our own

continent. Thus it is evident that such harmony of interests prevails in Europe at present that States can state in binding terms the prevailing situation and agree on the manner of further development of the conditions. In consequence, the principles agreed upon by the present Conference are not merely repeating what has been said before but, proceeding from an established basis, recognizing its value, they mean developing a new set of standards to open up new dimensions in the mutual relations of States.[35]

This is particularly true as regards the principle of self-determination. As has been argued, the Helsinki Declaration articulates a concept of self-determination that is different in many respects from that incorporated in the U.N. instruments. The Helsinki doctrine of self-determination reflects, to a very great extent, some of the basic tenets of the Western view of the concept; while the more recent U.N. statements tend to follow the gist of the socialist and Afro-Asian philosophy of self-determination (or at least could be so interpreted). This shift seems to be well-justified, for the latter concept is relevant to situations (colonialism or foreign or racist domination) which for the most part are nonexistent in Europe (or, for that matter, in North America). Thus, the new approach in the Helsinki Final Act is better suited to Euro-American conditions.

This new dimension is mainly one of political doctrine. In other words, the Helsinki Declaration has expanded and enriched the political philosophy behind the U.N. conception of self-determination by adding new values by which states should measure their conduct. However, this does not answer the question of what the impact of the Helsinki Declaration has been on the legal principles of self-determination. Could it be argued that it has no bearing at all on those legal principles? This question is too complex to be treated in great detail here,[36] but the following tentative observations seem to be warranted. Whenever the Helsinki Declaration does not restate or reaffirm legally binding international rules or principles, the "code of conduct" it requires[37] may have a dual effect. First, signatory states are made accountable for not complying with the standards of the Helsinki Declaration, although it cannot be said that disregard of the Helsinki Declaration amounts to an international delict. Second, signatory states, because of their adherence to the principles set forth in the Helsinki Declaration, are precluded from challenging the validity of the content given those principles in the Helsinki

Declaration. Put another way, the Helsinki Declaration has an estoppel effect as to principles it defines.

If this much is accepted, along with the legal rules on self-determination discussed previously, it can still be argued that states that have signed the Helsinki Declaration are not legally bound by Principle VIII but only by general international legal rules, which have a different scope and relevance. However, a signatory state could not claim that, when these legal rules have a different content, they would override the Helsinki Declaration or that the Helsinki Declaration must be construed in light of them. Signatory states are not freed from the political and moral duty to comply with the Helsinki Declaration.

Of course, if the 35 signatories consistently modify their behavior to comply with the Helsinki Declaration, then the customary law on self-determination and Principle VIII might tend to converge and even to amalgamate. This would, among other things, mean that Principle VIII would become legally binding, at least as to the 35 signatories, and this in turn would affect the entire scope of the customary and written law on self-determination, as it is applied to the entire international community.

NOTES

1. R. B. Russel, A HISTORY OF THE UNITED NATIONS CHARTER 811 (1958). See also G. Tunkin, THEORY OF INTERNATIONAL LAW, 62 (1974).

2. Hula, NATIONAL SELF-DETERMINATION RECONSIDERED, SOCIAL RESEARCH 1 (February 1943). The text of the statement made by Churchill to the House of Commons is reproduced in E. STETTINIUS, ROOSEVELT AND THE RUSSIANS: THE YALTA CONFERENCE 244-245 (1949).

3. See 6 DOCUMENTS OF THE U.N. CONFERENCE ON INTERNATIONAL ORGANIZATION, SAN FRANCISCO 1945, at 298 (1945).

4. See *Id., Report of Committee I to Commission I,* at 455.

5. It could be argued that, by referring to Germany and Italy, the framers of the U.N. Charter intended to refer to German and Italian abuse of plebiscites or similar forms of "alleged expression of the popular will," in cases of annexation of foreign countries. This interpretation, however, could only be valid for Germany (Nazi Germany resorted to plebiscites in the Saar in 1935 and in Austria in 1938; furthermore, it planned to organize a plebiscite in Czechoslovakia in 1938, which, however, was not carried out). By contrast, Fascist Italy did not use plebiscites or similar devices to give a legal justification to the takeover of other peoples or to other behavior of this kind. The 1939 agreements between Italy and Germany concerning Italian citizens of German descent living in South Tyrol provided for the right to opt for German nationality. This was clearly a right conferred on *individuals* (not on peoples or minorities) and *implied no territorial change* (as in the case of plebiscites).

The conclusion is, therefore, warranted that the reference to Italy and Germany made by the framers of the U.N. Charter and concerning self-determination was meant to point to the following: the authoritarian governments of those two states claimed to have been legitimized by "popular will" while, in fact, they were oppressive systems; they were not based on the "free and genuine" will of the people, but only on a legalistic and fictitious expression of that will.

6. For the socialist and the Afro-Asian view see Sahovic, *Influence des Etats nouveaux sur la conception du droit international,* ANNUAIRE FRANCAIS DE DROIT INTERNATIONAL, at 39-42 (1966); H. KOKOR-SEGO, NEW STATES AND INTERNATIONAL LAW, 11-51 (1970); R. ERICKSON, INTERNATIONAL LAW AND THE REVOLUTIONARY STATE, 55–77 (1972); G. TUNKIN, THEORY OF INTERNATIONAL LAW, above, note 1, at 60–69.

7. POEGGEL, in 1 VÖLKERRECHT (Manual of international law of the German Democratic Republic) 270 (1973) (translation mine).

8. *U.S. Urges Self-Determination for Peoples Everywhere,* DEPARTMENT OF STATE BULLETIN 740, at 741 (December 25, 1972).

9. Article 1 reads as follows: 1. All peoples have the right of self-determination. By virtue of that right they freely determine their political status and freely pursue their economic, social and cultural development. 2. All peoples may, for their own ends, freely dispose of their natural wealth and resources without prejudice to any obligations arising out of international economic co-operation, based upon the principle of mutual benefit, and international law. In no case may a people be deprived of its own means of subsistence. 3. The States Parties to the present Covenant, including those having responsibility for the administration of Non-Self-Governing and Trust Territories, shall promote the realization of the right of self-determination, and shall respect that right, in conformity with the provisions of the Charter of the United Nations.

10. F. CAPOTORTI, SAGGIO INTRODUTTIVO AI PATTI INTERNAZIONALI SUI DIRITTI DELL'UOMO, 24-25 (1967).

11. Rosenstock, *The Declaration of Principles of International Law Concerning Friendly Relations: a Survey,* 65 AM. J. OF INT'L L. 730 (1971); Arangio-Ruiz, *The Normative Role of the General Assembly of the United Nations and the Declaration of Principles on Friendly Relations,* RECUEIL DES COURS DE L'ACADÉMIE DE DROIT INTERNATIONAL, 565 (1972); Sinclair, *Principles of International Law Concerning Friendly Relations and Co-operation among States,* ESSAYS ON INTERNATIONAL LAW IN HONOUR OF K. RAO, 133 (1976).

12. Two points show the narrowing of self-determination to colonial or colonial-like situations. First, reference is made only to the need "to bring a speedy end to colonialism" and to the fact that "subjection of peoples to alien subjugation, domination and exploitation constitutes a violation of the principle" of self-determination. It can be noted, in passing, that the three words "subjugation," "domination," and "exploitation" are used conjunctively, as indicating cumulatively the same phenomenon. They are not referring to various forms of "alien control;" if this were the case, they would have too broad a scope, covering neo-colonialism or forms of indirect foreign oppression as well.

Secondly, the 1970 Declaration lists "the establishment of a sovereign and independent State" among the modes of implementing the right of self-determination. It follows that a people living in a sovereign state (say, the German people of the Federal Republic of Germany) could not claim the right of self-determination under the 1970 Declaration; for this right must be regarded as already implemented.

13. Paragraph 7 of the Principle on self-determination states:

Nothing in the foregoing paragraphs shall be construed as authorizing or encouraging any action which would dismember or impair, totally or in part, the territorial integrity or political *unity* of sovereign and independent States conducting themselves in compliance with the principle of equal rights and self-determination of peoples as described above and thus possessed of a government representing the whole people belonging to the territory without distinction as to race, creed or colour.

It could be argued that this clause is only intended to exclude the rights of peoples living in sovereign and nonracist states to disrupt the territorial integrity or political unity of the state; namely, the right to change the "external political status," while it conserves their right to other forms of self-determination (e.g., the right to pursue their economic, social, and cultural development). This contention, however, is not acceptable, for two reasons. First, it is clear that such narrowing of the right to self-determination would almost extinguish the right. Second, although the provision in question is couched ambiguously, as a "residual" or "safeguard" clause concerning only a single and specific problem (the possible conflict of self-determination with the demands of territorial integrity of sovereign states), it in fact gives a general definition of "independent and sovereign States conducting themselves in compliance with the principle of self-determination." It can therefore be held that the clause in question has a wide and general scope. It is intended to deal with the general question of whether peoples living in sovereign nonracist states can claim a right to self-determination, and gives a negative answer to this question.

14. As noted above, note 12, situations such as that of the German people are not covered by the U.N. Declaration on Friendly Relations, which leaves aside peoples of sovereign and independent countries (provided of course that the governments of these countries are not racist).

15. Russel, *The Helsinki Declaration: Brobdingnag or Liliput?* 70 AM. J. OF INT'L L. at 269 (1976).

16. Doc.CSCE/I/PV.3 at 26.

17. Doc.CSCE/I/3.

18. "By virtue of this principle, all peoples have the right to determine their own political status, *both internal and external, with complete freedom and without outside interference* and to pursue their economic, social and cultural development. Further, all states have a duty to respect this right. The participating states believe that respect for these principles should govern their relations with one another and should also characterize relationships among all states." (Editors' translation) Doc.CSCE/II/A/12 (emphasis added).

19. Doc.CSCE/I/28 (emphasis added).

20. Doc.CSCE/II/A/8 (emphasis added).

21. Doc.CSCE/I/PV.7 at 18-19.

22. Doc.CSCE/I/PV.6 at 83.

23. "The USSR objected to inclusion of a principle on self-determination in a Declaration enunciated by developed countries on the ground that self-determination has been traditionally associated with the right of colonial peoples to establish their independence." Russel, above, note 15.

24. See respectively Doc.CSCE/I/PV.3 at 87 and III/PV.4 at 40 (Spain) and Doc.CSCE/I/PV.6 at 82-83 and III/PV.3 at 20 (Ireland).

25. See Doc.CSCE/I/PV.6 at 26, PV.7 at 29-30; Doc.CSCE/III/PV.3 at 24; PV.4 at 12.

26. "States with militant minorities, such as Canada and Yugoslavia, felt the need for a 'balancing element,' which was a euphemism for a limit to the application of the principle to national minorities in order to avoid any implication that the principle could be used to bring about the dissolution of federated States comprised of peoples of different nationalities or other minorities." Russel, above, note 15, at 269-270.

27. Doc.CSCE/III/PV.5 at 17.

28. See for example the declarations of the foreign ministers of the Netherlands and Ireland, quoted above, notes 22 and 23.

29. Doc.CSCE/III/PV.1 at 5 (emphasis added).

30. *Id.*

31. Greece, *Id.,* PV.2 at 10.

32. Ireland, *Id.,* PV.3 at 21-22.

33. German Democratic Republic, *Id.,* at 25.

34. Ireland, *Id.,* PV.3 at 21.

35. Doc.CSCE/III/PV.4 at 34.

36. On this question see among others, Schachter, *The Twilight Existence of Non-binding International Agreements,* 71 AM. J. OF INT'L L. at 296 (1977).

37. This expression was used by the Soviet Union (Doc.CSCE/I/PV.2 at 5) and by the United Kingdom (*Id.,* PV.5 at 9-10).

7 The Implementation of the Human Rights Provisions of the Helsinki Final Act A Preliminary Assessment: 1975–1977

by VIRGINIA LEARY

The approach of the Belgrade Conference two years after the signing of the Helsinki Final Act is an appropriate moment for a preliminary assessment of the implementation of the human rights provisions of the Final Act. In the brief period since the Final Act was adopted, an extraordinary number of studies, articles, and comments concerning implementation, particularly of the human rights provisions, have appeared.

Much of this concern has been stimulated by the Belgrade conference, where implementation will be discussed; but it also appears to result from the widespread publication of the entire text of the Final Act in Eastern Europe and the emphasis on the human rights provisions in the Western press. It reflects a conviction that the participating states cannot be relied upon to implement effectively the moral pledges they made at Helsinki and that an informed public opinion is required to focus attention on human rights at the Belgrade conference. The extent to which the Final Act is being cited in connection with specific human rights situations is extraordinary in view of its agreed nonbinding nature. It appears to have taken on greater significance as a standard for human rights in the mind of the general public than have the binding provisions of the U.N. covenants. A development reminiscent of the citation of the Universal Declaration of Human Rights seems to be occurring, investing a nonbinding document with a living reality.

A number of problems are apparent in assessing implementation of the Helsinki Accord at this early stage. Two years is an extremely short period in which to evaluate the implementation of a long-term agreement. Expectations concerning implementation, therefore, should be limited to what could reasonably be accomplished in such a brief period. In addition, the evaluation is difficult because of the heterogeneous nature of the human rights provisions. Principle VII contains general language concerning respect for human rights, while Basket III contains specific commitments. This makes it relatively easy to determine whether steps have been taken to implement Basket III, but difficult to assess implementation of Principle VII which, together with the provisions of Basket I, "contains enough generalities and other loopholes to rationalize substantial noncompliance by unwilling states."[1] Finally, it is clear that the signatory states have given different interpretations to the same provisions so that they "have at times sought to win through reinterpretation points lost in the negotiation."[2] The different connotations given by the signatory states to "freedom of information" especially illustrate this problem.

With the above difficulties in mind, it nevertheless remains possible, on the basis of the extensive information available, to arrive at a preliminary evaluation. While public attention has focused on certain failures to implement the human rights provisions, it is evident that the Helsinki Conference has served as a stimulus for some positive action in this field, as the information in this chapter illustrates. The chapter itself is divided into two parts. The first reports on the numerous government, semi-official, and private efforts to monitor the human rights provisions; the findings of these monitoring groups; and reactions to their activities. The second part deals with the particular problem areas of human contacts, freedom of information, cultural exchange, and religious liberty. It attempts to assess the degree of implementation in each of these specific areas.

MONITORING OF THE IMPLEMENTATION OF THE HELSINKI HUMAN RIGHTS PROVISIONS

No provision is made in the Final Act for permanent machinery to supervise implementation. Participating states simply "declare their resolve, in the period following the Conference to pay due regard to and implement the provisions of the Final Act of the Conference.'' They agree to meet together in Belgrade in 1977 and in subsequent meetings for ''a thorough exchange of views both on the implementation of the Final Act and of the tasks defined by the Conference.'' This vacuum in the implementation of the human rights provisions has thus been filled by government spokesmen, intergovernmental organizations, parliamentary commissions, informal monitoring groups, and religious organizations which have undertaken to investigate the implementation of the Final Act.

Monitoring by Governments and Semi-Official Groups

Monitoring by participating states. While monitoring by private groups and by individuals may be considered unofficial, the participating states in the Helsinki conference obviously have a special right to speak out concerning implementation of the Final Act. And they have done so on many occasions, both individually and within organizations such as the Council of Europe and the Inter-Parliamentary Union. President Carter has stated that the U.S. has a ''responsibility and a legal right'' to speak out on human rights violations as one of the signatory nations of the Helsinki agreement. In a news conference on February 23, 1977, the President said:

> We are a signatory of the Helsinki Agreement. We are ourselves culpable in some ways for not giving people adequate right to move around our country or restricting, unnecessarily in my opinion, visitation to this country by those who disagree with us politically.[3]

On January 26, 1977, the U.S. State Department for the first time publicly criticized a government for failure to live up to the Helsinki Accord. The criticism concerned Charter 77, a petition to the government of Czechoslovakia eventually signed by nearly 700 individuals and citing numerous violations of human rights in that country. The State Department release cited the human rights principle of the Helsinki agreement and stated, ''All signatories of the Helsinki Final Act are pledged to promote, respect and observe human rights and fundamental freedoms for all. We must strongly deplore the violation of such rights and freedoms wherever they occur.''[4]

On February 7, 1977, a spokesman for the State Department referred to the arrest of Alexander Ginsburg, a member of the Helsinki monitoring group in the U.S.S.R.

> Wherever it may occur, the harassment of individuals who are pursuing the principle set forth in the Universal Declaration of Human Rights, or who are working for the implenentation of the Final Act of the Helsinki Conference is a matter of profound concern for all Americans. [5]

In addition to these remarks by U.S. government representatives, much more detailed analyses regarding implementation are contained in the two reports of the U.S. President to the Congressional Commission on Security and Cooperation in Europe (December 1976 and June 1977). Specific information from these reports will be cited later. Although the first report states that the U.S. has monitored the implementation activity of all the participating states, it focuses on implementation in Eastern Europe. The letter of former President Ford, transmitting the report to the Congressional Commission states:

> In the vitally important humanitarian and related fields, progress has been both limited and uneven. Predictably the most difficult areas have involved human contacts and the freer flow of information, concepts in the practical implementation of which the Soviet Union and its Eastern European Allies continue to have ideas very different from the West. There have been some positive developments in the fields of culture and education, which again build upon experiences which predate the Helsinki Summit. It is evident, however, that so far the Soviet and East European record on human rights remains inadequate when measured against the important undertakings of the Helsinki Final Act. The success of the Belgrade meeting will depend primarily on constructive Eastern efforts in the period ahead. [6]

In February 1977, Louis de Guiringaud, the French foreign minister, showed a preference for quiet diplomatic action as the best means of implementing human rights. In referring to the refusal of President Giscard d'Estaing to see the exiled Soviet dissident Andrei Amalrik, he stated that the best way to promote human rights was by diplomatic action to achieve compliance with the pledges contained in the Helsinki Accords rather than by joining a demonstration led by Mr. Amalrik. [7] Mr. Amalrik had attempted to enter the Elysee Palace to see the President and had been seized by police. He carried a placard reading, "Demand Application of the Helsinki Accords."

In his first major speech the British foreign secretary, David Owen, praised the human rights pledges in the Helsinki Final Act, but, alluding to Charter 77, stated that "on the whole there had been little progress toward carrying out the Accords."[8]

The Parliamentary Assembly of the Council of Europe held two debates in 1976 and 1977, in which it discussed a number of reports on the implementation of the Final Act, including the human rights and humanitarian provisions.[9] Discussions concerning implementation have also been carried on within NATO.

Concerning comments on implementation, which focused to a great extent on violations of human rights in Eastern Europe, the Soviet press reacted strongly. It saw in the allegations an attempt to "poison the atmosphere of international relations" on the threshold of the Belgrade meeting and cited the principle of nonintervention. It was emphasized frequently that the question of implementation at Belgrade must focus on all aspects of the Helsinki Accord and not only on the human rights and humanitarian provisions. In addition, reference was made to Western political figures who questioned the strong human rights stand taken by President Carter in particular.

In February 1977, the head of the U.S.S.R. Ministry of Foreign Affairs Press Department said:

> Many persons in the West, including Cyrus Vance, the new U.S. Secretary of State, are saying that Washington should keep a close watch on how the USSR is carrying out the terms of the Helsinki Conference's Final Act. Our answers to those persons is that no one has given you the right to check up on others, especially when the others are independent, sovereign states. If you want to exchange opinions, that's another matter.[10]

In further comments, he referred to the U.S.S.R.'s fulfillment of Basket II provisions and stated that the Soviet Union was far ahead of the "so-called Western democratic" countries in the implementation of the provisions of Basket III relating to the study of foreign languages, the publication of foreign literature, showings of foreign films and TV programs, and imports of foreign publications. He also explained the improved facilities offered foreign journalists. Although the U.S.S.R. has on many occasions referred to violations of human rights in the West, citing specific instances of such violations, they have not linked such violations expressly to the Helsinki agreements. This appears to be in keeping with their interpretation of the Final Act. One exception is a reference to the "witch hunt" being carried out in the Federal Republic of Germany (referring to the requirements of extensive security clearance for employment in the government in West Germany and the dismissal of certain employees from government jobs). A *Pravda* article quotes the West German magazine *Stern* as saying that "A member of a neo-Nazi Party can be a state employee but a Communist has to remain on the outside." The *Pravda* article also stated that: "Such actions are also at variance with the Final Act of the all-European Conference in Helsinki."[11]

According to the *Current Digest of the Soviet Press:*

> Throughout the week, *Pravda* and *Izvestia* focused an unusual amount of attention (several articles daily) on violations of human rights in the non-socialist world, chiefly in countries that are the traditional targets of Soviet criticism. Both papers carried daily reports on the proceedings of the European Commission on Human Rights in Strasbourg, at which the Irish Republic accused the United Kingdom of torturing prisoners in Northern Ireland in violation of the European Convention on Human Rights. Other countries criticized for human rights violations were: Israel, which is currently being investigated by the UN Commission on Human Rights in Geneva for its actions in the occupied territories; South Africa, for the detention of political prisoners in intolerable conditions on Robben Island; the United States for turning on official blind eye to the illegal immigration and subsequent mistreatment of Mexican and other Latin American workers; France where industries receive police assistance in blacklisting trade union activists; Chile, Paraguay and others.[12]

Monitoring by Parliament and Political Parties. There have been numerous references to the implementation of the Helsinki Final Act in various parliaments. The Inter-Parliamentary Union, which includes parliamentarians from both East and West Europe, has carried out an intensive study of implementation of the Final Act and has issued several reports on the subject.[13] The European Parliament passed a resolution charging the U.S.S.R. with ignoring the human rights provisions of the Helsinki agreement by the imprisonment of Vladimir Bukovsky for anti-soviet agitation.[14] The *Congressional Record* of the U.S. Senate and House of Representatives contains comments and resolutions too numerous to cite, referring to human rights violations of the Final Act, particularly in Eastern Europe.

Communist parties in Western Europe have also commented on implementation. The *New York Times* reported on March 4, 1977, in a dispatch from Madrid, that

> The leaders of the Spanish, Italian and French Communist parties called today for the "full application" of the Helsinki Accords, which included pledges by both Eastern and Western countries of respect for human rights. But the three leaders did not specifically mention recent attacks on dissidents in the Soviet bloc countries. . . The failure of the joint communique to mention the repression of movements for human rights in Communist Europe was something of a setback for Mr. Carrillo (of the Spanish Party) who had originally hoped that the Madrid gathering would endorse his maverick party's outspoken stand on the issue. . . Asked to explain the silence on the rights issue, Mr. Marchais (French party) recalled past disputes among Communist parties—such as the Soviet Union's "excommunication" of Yugoslavia and efforts to isolate China—and said the three Western European parties wanted to avoid others.[15]

According to a Reuters dispatch of April 17, 1977, Western European socialist leaders, including former Chancellor Willy Brandt of West Germany, agreed to "keep pressing the Soviet bloc to respect human rights, saying their aim was fully compatible with détente".[16] The discussions on human rights were apparently brought up in the context of preparations for the Belgrade Conference.

Perhaps one of the most substantial efforts by national legislative organs to monitor the Helsinki agreements has been the setting up in the U.S. of a congressional Commission on Security and Cooperation in Europe, commonly referred to as the Helsinki Commission. The idea for the commission originated from a trip which several congressional leaders made to the Soviet Union immediately after the Helsinki Final Act had been signed. One of the congresswomen reported that

> During our travel in the USSR, the congressional delegation found many Soviet citizens hopeful that the Accord would finally help them obtain a measure of freedom in the USSR, or would give them means to leave and find freedom elsewhere . . . . Through all our conversations, the one consistent thread was that the West must not forget the third basket of the Helsinki Accord which addresses itself to

human rights. . . . When we met with Mr. Brezhnev we spoke to him about this and rather resignedly he sighed and said this was the 150th time the basket three provisions had been brought to his attention and he pointed out there would be an international commission meeting in Belgrade in October 1977. That commission, I'm sorry to say, will only begin to study ways in which these accords can be monitored. So it's quite a long way from any implementation.[17]

The U.S. Helsinki Commission was subsequently created. It consisted of six members of the House of Representatives, six senators and three representativies of the executive branch of the government (from the Departments of State, Defense, and Commerce). Its purpose is to monitor acts of the Helsinki signatory countries with regard to compliance with the provisions of the Final Act, particularly the humanitarian provisions.

Its less official purpose appears to be to maintain a certain pressure on the executive branch. The deputy staff director of the commission, on December 1, 1976, stated: "Only if American public opinion presses the American government to seek real progress on the human rights promises of the Final Act can we expect American officials even to raise such questions at the diplomatic level."[18]

The setting up of the Helsinki Commission had been considered inadvisable by the executive branch. In a letter to the chairman of the House of Representatives committee considering the legislation to create the commission, a representative of the State Department explained that the State Department itself was monitoring implementation of the Helsinki Accords, that it was regularly exchanging information with U.S. allies within the framework of NATO concerning compliance, and had taken up with the Soviet Union a number of questions concerning problems of implementation. The letter concluded,

The commission envisaged . . . would not appear to be equipped to add significantly to the action already being taken or the information being compiled; nor would it appear able to exercise a more effective monitoring role than existing committees or subcommittees of the Congress. Furthermore, its extraordinary composition would not seem to provide an appropriate or effective means for coordinating or guiding our efforts. In sum, we share the interest of the sponsors of these bills in effective monitoring of CSCE implementation, but do not believe the proposed commission would add to the efforts and procedures already established. Therefore, the Department of State recommends against enactment of this legislation.[19]

Subsequently, under the Carter administration, relations between the executive branch and the commission improved.

The Helsinki Commission has come to play an important role in alerting the U.S. public to the question of implementation of the Helsinki Final Act and in focusing attention on human rights violations, a role which it is highly unlikely the State Department could have played. At the same time it has greatly irritated the Soviet Union by its concentration on human rights violations within Eastern Europe. The commission has held public hearings both to acquire information and to promote implementation. Hearings have been held on family reunification, on the freer flow of information and the expansion of educational and cultural exchanges, and specifically on Helsinki compliance in Eastern Europe. Most recently, it attracted widespread press attention when Rudolph Nureyev testified before the commission concerning his mother's unsuccessful efforts in the Soviet Union to obtain a visa to visit him. It has become a focal point for individuals and nongovernmental organizations concerned with implementation of the Helsinki Accords; many persons have channeled information to the commission.

The Helsinki Commission sent a study mission to Europe in December 1976,

> to gather information about the current status of implementation of the provisions of the Helsinki Accords and to establish contacts with key European political and governmental officials as well as private individuals and organizations concerned with various aspects of the implementation process.[20]

The members of the study mission visited 18 signatory countries. However, the Warsaw Pact countries refused to permit the members of the study mission to visit. The *Report* of the study mission stated that this was "an action which runs counter to the very spirit of Helsinki."[21]

The Soviet view of the Helsinki Commission was stated in *Pravda:*

> . . .Washington unilaterally created a Congressional "monitoring" commission to check up on fulfillment of the Final Act's third section. Things reached a point at which this self-styled "commission" tried to stage an "inspection" in the socialist countries, an action that demonstrated once again the high-handed attitude of the cold war champions in the U.S. Congress toward the sovereignty of other states

and at the same time toward the Final Act, which lists non-interference in internal affairs as one of the 10 basic principles of relations between the states participating in the all-European Conference. . . . Thus, the line of the West's reactionary circles with respect to the Belgrade meeting is clearly drawn—it is a line having very little in common with a genuine desire to carry out all aspects of the Final Act or to consolidate and develop international cooperation. This is a dangerous line. Enormous efforts were required to achieve an easing of international tension, to convene the 35-state conference and to bring it to a favorable conclusion. Any attempts to do away with or distort the Accords reached there, which are an important possession of the peoples, should be firmly condemned.[22]

Reportedly, in retaliation for the U.S.S.R.'s refusal to grant visas to the Helsinki Commission, the U.S. denied an entry visa to Alexander Chakovsky, editor of *Literary Gazette* and a member of the official Soviet committee on the Helsinki Accords.[23]

The *Report* of the Study Mission to Europe contained a number of remarks concerning implementation of the Helsinki Final Act. After referring to the provisions relating to reunification of families, accrediting journalists, freedom of information, and treatment of ethnic minorities it stated:

No government spokesman with whom the Study Mission talked claimed that progress in any of these areas—except, with certain Eastern countries, family reunification—had been significant. All, however, pointed out that such subjects would have been beyond the diplomatic pale without Helsinki.[24]

The *Report* continued:

Less tangibly, the Accords were seen to have had a deterrent effect on Communist states in their behavior toward their own citizens as well as outsiders. Several non-governmental experts on Eastern European and Soviet affairs pointed to the obvious sensitivity of the Communist nations on Helsinki-related issues as a sign of the restraint the Accords impose. Government officials, moreover, reported actual instances where junior communist functionaries had advised their seniors that a contemplated course of action was barred by the Helsinki understandings. Such deterrence is obviously extremely hard to document. It is very difficult to prove a negative. Nevertheless, the Study Mission was impressed by the sober assessment of qualified observers of Communist affairs about the deterrent effect the Accords are having on some forms of repression at home and ambition abroad. . . Of the appeals for recognition and support received in the

West from Soviet dissenters—religious, political, ethnic, individual—almost all base their case against the Soviet authorities on the principles and provisions of the Helsinki Accords.[25]

Unofficial Monitoring

National monitoring groups of private individuals. National groups have been set up in several European countries to monitor the Helsinki Accord. The *Manchester Guardian Weekly,* on March 20, 1977, carried a letter from the Rt. Hon. George Thomson announcing the setting up of a study group of 21 people in the United Kingdom to assess the results of the Helsinki Final Act. There was no reference to a focus on the human rights or humanitarian provisions. The group issued an interim report, in June 1977, and plans to issue a final report, in September 1977, to coincide with the second Belgrade conference.[26]

On May 12, the Public Group to Promote Observance of the Helsinki Accords in the U.S.S.R. (commonly called the "Helsinki Watch Group") was founded with 11 members under the chairmanship of the physicist Yuri Orlov. It intends to foster compliance with the humanitarian provisions of the Final Act. Its first public statement said:

The Group considers that its most urgent task is to inform all Heads of States signatory to the Final Act of August 1, 1975, and the public at large of direct violations of the provisions mentioned above. In this regard the Group:

1) will accept directly from Soviet citizens written complaints which concern them personally and which relate to the (humanitarian) provisions. . . . The Group will forward such complaints in abridged form to all Heads of States signatory to the Final Act and will inform the public at large of the substance of the complaints. The Group will retain the original complaint signed by the author;

2) will gather, with the assistance of the public, other information on violations of the provisions mentioned above, organize this information, evaluate its reliability and forward it to Heads of States and to the public. When the Group encounters specific information on flagrant acts of inhumanity such as:

—taking children from the custody of religious parents who wish to rear their children in their own faith;

—compulsory psychiatric treatment for the purpose of altering a person's thought, conscience, religion or belief;

—dramatic instances of separation of families;

—extremely brutal treatment of prisoners of conscience.

The Group intends to appeal to Heads of State and to the public to form international commissions to verify such information on the spot, since it will not always be possible for the Group to verify such crucial information directly.   The Group hopes that its information will be taken into account at the official meetings called for in the section of the Final Act entitled "Follow up to the Conference."

The Group's members are inspired in their activities by the conviction that humanitarian problems and freedom of information have a direct bearing on international security. We appeal to the public of the other participating states to form national groups to promote complete fulfillment of the Helsinki agreements by the governments of their own countries.   We hope that a corresponding International Committee will also be organized in the future.[27]

On May 27, 1976, in an open appeal to the governments and parliaments of the Helsinki signatory states, Yuri Orlov announced that the Helsinki Watch Group in the U.S.S.R. had been declared an "illegal organization" and "an unconstitutional organization engaged in provocations." He reported:

Numerous KGB agents almost demonstratively follow my steps and the steps of other Group members, evidently in expectation of an order for our arrest. . . . If the collection and transmission of information on violations of these provisions are classified as crimes against the state, then this undermines the very basis of the Accords and deprives them of real content and internal consistency. Therefore I appeal to the governments and parliaments of all the states participating in the European Conference, including the USSR. I ask them to take steps which will protect the right of the Group to Promote Observance of the Helsinki Accords to function in a reasonable and constructive fashion in conformity with its stated purpose. I ask them to protect the members of the Group against persecution.[28]

On February 10, 1977, an article in the Western press reported:

In perhaps the most significant move yet in the current crackdown on dissidents, Soviet authorities today arrested Yuri Orlov, leader of an unofficial group that has been monitoring Kremlin compliance with human rights provisions of the Helsinki Accord. . . . The arrest was the fourth since Friday involving the Helsinki monitoring group. . . with the Belgrade conference scheduled in June to assess the results of the Helsinki Accord, Moscow plainly wants to stifle voices that will argue that Soviet compliance with the document has been minimal.[29]

Numerous protests were voiced in the West following these arrests. The U.S. State Department, which had earlier issued a statement of concern over the arrest of Alexander Ginsburg, another member of the Soviet monitoring group, made no public comment on the arrest of Orlov because, it was reported, "of a decision by Secretary of State Vance that continued public statements to the press would lose their force."[30] State Department officials did say, however, that the U.S. delegate to the U.N. Commission on Human Rights (then in session) had been instructed to propose an investigation by the commission into the arrest of Mr. Orlov and to state the U.S. concern. A resolution to this effect was presented by the U.S. to the Commission on Human Rights, but was withdrawn when it became clear that it would not be approved.

Other Helsinki monitoring groups were set up in the Ukraine, Lithuania, and Romania. In Poland, a new human rights organization was created, but it did not call itself a Helsinki monitoring group and apparently is emphasizing the U.N. covenants rather than the Helsinki Accord as a standard for human rights. In Czechoslovakia, Charter 77 was issued citing the Helsinki agreement.

These monitoring groups issued statements at various times citing specific violations of human rights in Eastern Europe. On July 22, 1976, the U.S.S.R. Helsinki Watch Group issued a 13-page report charging violations of the Helsinki Accord in a number of specific instances in the U.S.S.R. These included violations of postal and telephone communications, conditions of detention of political prisoners, separation of families, and repression against religious families.[31]

On February 12, immediately following Orlov's arrest, an editorial appeared in *Pravda* reporting the Soviet view of these activities:

It is also no accident that bourgeois ideologists and the direct executors of their will in the press and on radio and television have enlisted the services of "dissidents"—or, in plainer terms, renegades. This lends bourgeois propaganda a semblance of "objectivity" and more important, creates an even more illusory semblance that some kind of "opposition" to the socialist system exists. In fact, the overt opponents of socialism are an insignificant little group of people who do not represent anyone or anything, are remote from the Soviet people and exist only because they are supported, paid and extolled by the West. . . . The truth is that in the Soviet Union no one is per-secuted for his beliefs. But, in accordance with Soviet laws, charges may be brought against individuals who engage in anti-Soviet propaganda and agitation aimed at undermining or weakening the social and political system established in our country or who engage in the systematic dissemination of fabrications, which they know are false, defaming the Soviet state and social system. Thus, what we are talking about here is the penalties for deliberate actions provided in Articles 70 and 190 of the Russian Republic Criminal Code and the corresponding articles of the other Union republics' criminal codes.[32]

In July 1977, while the first session of the Belgrade Conference was going on, Alexander Ginsburg, one of the members of the U.S.S.R. Helsinki Watch Group, was convicted of anti-Soviet agitation and propaganda. As a "repeated offender," he was liable to a sentence of 10 years imprisonment. In June 1977, on the eve of the first Belgrade conference, it was reported that nine of the 11 original members of the Helsinki Watch Group in the U.S.S.R. had been arrested.

In early 1977, Charter 77, a manifesto concerning human rights in Czechoslovakia, was published over the signatures of 300 people. The name "Charter 77" was chosen "on the threshold of what has been declared the year of political prisoners, in the course of which a meeting in Belgrade is to review the progress—or lack of it—achieved since the Helsinki Conference."[33]

Although the Helsinki Final Act was prominent in the consciousness of the signers of Charter 77, as is evidenced by the reasons for the choice of the title, the provisions of the two U.N. Covenants on Human Rights were used as the standard against which to measure the degree of freedom in Czechoslovakia. Citations of violations of human rights were related to specific articles of the covenants.

When it was reported that many of the signers of Charter 77 were being harassed and detained, the U.S. State Department charged that Czechoslovakia was violating the provisions of the Helsinki agreement. (The text of this State Department release has been given above at page 113.)

On March 16, Reuters news agency reported from Prague:

Jan Patocka, the Czechoslovak campaigner for human rights, was buried here today in rites attended by a thousand mourners and a hundred plainclothes policemen. Professor Patocka . . . was stricken a week after having been interrogated by the police for 11 hours, mainly about a meeting he had had with the visiting Dutch Foreign Minister, Max van der Stoel.[34]

The news release mentioned that Professor Patocka was one of the three principal sponsors of Charter 77, together with Vaclev Havel, a playwright, and Jiri Hajek, foreign minister under the Dubcek administration. The playwright was reported to be in prison and the former foreign minister under house arrest.

An appeal was made in February by nine Romanians, asking the help of the signatory states of the Helsinki Final Act in obtaining increased respect for human rights in Romania. Some of the signers of the appeal, including Paul Goma, a prominent novelist, were subsequently harassed and arrested.

Monitoring by nongovernmental human rights organizations.
Some international human rights organizations, such as Amnesty International and the International Commission of Jurists, while continuing their very active work in defense of human rights, have not placed special emphasis on the provisions of the Helsinki Agreement. Others, such as the International League for Human Rights, have made frequent reference to the Helsinki Final Act in relation to specific human rights problems.

During 1975 and 1976, and up to mid-1977, the League wrote nearly 20 letters to governments in Eastern Europe citing the Helsinki human rights and humanitarian provisions in connection with particular human rights problems. In October 1975, the League wrote to Secretary of State Kissinger in connection with the U.S. government's refusal to grant visas to Sergio Segre, an official of the Communist Party of Italy, who had been invited to speak before the Council on Foreign Relations, and Hugo Blanco, a Peruvian author, who had been invited to lecture by several leading universities and organizations. The letter stated:

While we recognize the right of the United States Government under the law to deny admission to these persons, we desire to inquire whether the policy of the United States has been at all changed by the Helsinki agreements between Western and Eastern states. We would assume from its language that the United States as well as the Soviet Union would ease the restrictions imposed by both countries on admissions. May we ask as a matter of international policy what the effect of these agreements are on United States practices. We are aware that the ban is not absolute and that a certain amount of discretion may be exercised by United States officials.[35]

The League has also been extremely active in cases involving family reunification, a subject specifically covered in the Helsinki Agreement. In connection with such cases, they have written a number of letters to Eastern and Western European countries and have sent a detailed report on three cases of family separations to the U.S. congressional Helsinki Commission in connection with its hearings on that problem. They have also been investigating the breakdown in postal communications between Western countries and the U.S.S.R. Their files have shown a rather serious percentage of nondelivery of mail in particular cases.

Jewish human rights organizations have also been particularly active in monitoring the implementation of the Helsinki agreement because of their concern about the emigration of Jews from the Soviet Union and the treatment of Jews in general in Eastern Europe. They have published articles and studies on the Helsinki agreement and its relation to emigration and reunification of families and have provided information on the subject to other Helsinki monitoring groups.

On hearing of the project of the American Society of International Law on implementation of the Helsinki Accord, the American Civil Liberties Union (the U.S. organization most active in the field of human rights) provided the author of this paper with all their current documentation on U.S. human rights problems. The documentation does not, however, contain specific reference to commitments made by the U.S. at Helsinki.

The preceding discussion of monitoring groups is clearly not exhaustive. Many other organizations and individuals play an active role in monitoring the Helsinki Final Act. The European Cooperation Research Group in London has published several reports on the implementation of the Helsinki Accord. Three research institutes in England, Switzerland, and the Netherlands have prepared a joint report on "Religious Liberty in the Soviet Union." They have submitted the report to the World Council of Churches (WCC), which itself is conducting a current inquiry into religious liberty in the 35 Helsinki states.

It is apparent that most of the monitoring groups, both in Western and Eastern Europe, have concentrated on failures of implementation in Eastern Europe, although replies to the World Council of Churches inquiries on Helsinki implementation contain many reports of human rights violations in Western countries from the churches in these countries. There are a number of explanations for this concentration on Eastern Europe. Human rights organizations have long been active in the West, monitoring human rights violations in their own countries with reference to constitutional or philosophical principles of civil liberty long accepted—theoretically at least—in the West. It apparently has seemed unnecessary to such groups to relate human rights problems in their own country to international standards, such as those in the Helsinki Accord. At any rate, they have been very slow to do so. In the United States, however a number of journalists and others, including President Carter, have criticized the restrictive U.S. policy on visas for visitors as being contrary to the spirit of the Helsinki Final Act. Nevertheless, it is rare to find Helsinki monitoring groups in the West which concentrate on violations of human rights by their own governments.

PROBLEM AREAS IN THE IMPLEMENTATION
OF THE HELSINKI ACCORDS

Human Contacts

In Basket III, the participating states expressed the intention to "make it their aim to facilitate freer movements and contacts, individually and collectively, whether privately or officially among persons, institutions and organizations of the participating States and to contribute to the solution of the humanitarian problems that arise in that connection." Other paragraphs of this section of the Accord refer to facilitating reunification of families, marriages between citizens of different states, travel for personal or professional reasons, tourism, meetings among young people, sports, and expansion of contacts among governmental institutions and nongovernmental organizations and associations.

The U.S. President's *Second Semi-Annual Report* to the Helsinki Commission stated,

Despite some apparent efforts to improve the implementation records for the Belgrade review meeting, the Warsaw countries have not fundamentally altered their policies on human contacts during the reporting period. Most Soviet and Eastern European officials continued to view travel or emigration to the West as a privilege to be granted or refused by the state rather than as a matter of personal choice.[36]

Travel restrictions. The U.S. began a review of its visa procedures following the Helsinki Conference. President Carter's remarks that U.S. visa requirements should be reconsidered in the light of the Helsinki Final Act have been referred to previously. In March 1977, the U.S. lifted restrictions on the use of U.S. passports for travel to Cuba, North Korea, Vietnam, and Cambodia.[37] An article in *Le Monde Diplomatique* in June 1977, part of a series on implementation of the Helsinki Accord, called attention to the remnants of McCarthyism still inscribed in U.S. immigration legislation.[38] The article points out that the 1952 immigration law (the McCarran-Walter Act), while permitting exceptions to be made by the State Department, forbids entry to the U.S.—even for visits—of anarchists, communists or other persons engaged in subversive activities. It reports that the 1952 law has been applied over the years to bar entry to Communist Party members from a number of Western countries as well as other "suspect" persons who were not communists. The article concludes, "As long as the doors of the United States are closed to foreign visitors of different ideologies and the McCarran Act is not purely and simply repealed, how is it possible for the United States to invoke the principles of the Helsinki Conference?"[39]

In April 1977, the U.S. State Department refused visas to three Soviet trade unionists who wanted to attend a labor convention in the United States to which they had been invited.[40] The official Soviet news agency, TASS, commented that this action violated the Helsinki provisions on international contacts.[41] Similar Soviet protests had been made earlier over the denial of visas to Soviet labor leaders. The U.S. position on the question is expressed in the president's first report to the Helsinki Commission:

The last paragraph of the Human Contacts section of Basket Three calls for further development of contacts among governmental institutions and non-governmental organizations of the participating states. This provision, which was included in the Final Act on the initiative of the Eastern side, has been invoked by the Soviets to protest the fact that Soviet labor representatives have not received visas to visit the United States. The Soviet labor representatives were refused visas under the terms of the Immigration and Naturalization Act regarding Communist Party membership. Waivers of ineligibility were not recommended, in keeping with long-standing policy in such cases. The views of the American labor movement were taken into consideration in this decision. *Moreover, specific reference to travel and contacts among labor representatives does not appear in the Final Act because of the U.S. position on the subject.* All participants were aware of our long-standing policy, and, in signing the Final Act, had accepted our position against a reference to such exchanges.[42]

The U.S. action in banning the Soviet trade unionists has been criticized both within and without the U.S. (including by the author of the article *Le Monde Diplomatique*) as contrary to the Helsinki Accord.

As mentioned previously, the U.S. denied a visa to a member of the official Soviet Committee on the Helsinki Accord in retaliation for the U.S.S.R.'s refusal to grant visas to the members of the Study Mission of the congressional Helsinki Commission. This action raises the interesting question whether retaliation is an acceptable method of implementing the Helsinki Final Act. The question has also arisen in the context of the expulsion of a TASS correspondent in the U.S. in retaliation for the expulsion of an Associated Press correspondent in Moscow. In the present state of international affairs and in the absence of an agreed method of implementing international agreements, retaliation remains one of the few recourses in cases of violations. On the other hand, it scarcely seems in keeping with the spirit of Helsinki to retaliate in kind to a violation of a humanitarian provision.

The interim report of the United Kingdom Helsinki Review Group, in reviewing travel restrictions in the Soviet Union, states:

Claims that vast numbers of Soviet citizens now travel abroad must be viewed with some scepticism: few travel except in very large parties; and a large proportion visit only the other countries of Eastern Europe. There remains an imbalance between the number of tourists from, for example, the United Kingdom who visit Eastern Europe and the number of Eastern European tourists who visit the United Kingdom . . . . There remain many restrictions on travel (in the Soviet Union) once entry visas have been granted. "Due regard for security requirements" is written into the Final Act but many of the restrictions could be eased or lifted. Although there are persistent complaints from East European governments about delays by Western governments over the issuing of visas, once they have been granted travel is unrestricted.[43]

The report also cites criticism of the U.S. immigration restrictions. It adds, "The United Kingdom is also the subject of criticisms. British procedures remain slow and cumbersome: for example, it was not until December 1976 that reciprocal visa proposals were made by the United Kingdom to Eastern European countries.[44] The WCC has found that Eastern churchmen have greater difficulty obtaining visas for Western countries than Western churchmen have in obtaining visas for Eastern countries.

Family reunification.   One of the more specific provisions of Basket III concerns the reunification of families. It provides, *inter alia,* that participating states "will deal in a positive and humanitarian spirit" with the application of persons who wish to be reunited with members of their families, that applications in this field should be dealt with expeditiously, and that fees in connection with these applications should be maintained at a moderate level. The rather precise formulation of these provisions has made monitoring implementation somewhat easier than in the case of other provisions. As a result, there is a considerable amount of information available regarding implementation on family reunification.

A problem has arisen concerning the definition of "family." No definition had been given in the act itself, apparently because the Western States believe that a precise definition might turn out to be a justification for limiting emigration. Nevertheless, the absence of definition has led to controversy about whether these provisions are being implemented or not. In granting and denying visas for family reunion it has been alleged that the Soviet Union has given a narrow interpretation to family. "In June 1976 Vladimir Obidin, head of OVIR, stated that reunification of family provisions applied only to spouses and their unmarried children, leading to refusals of exit visas on grounds of 'an insufficient degree of kinship. . . . ' There are reports that in some areas of the USSR, Soviet officials are interpreting more strictly the definition of 'family' for emigration purposes. If this reported practice continues and is adopted throughout the U.S.S.R., it could have serious implications for reunification of families under the CSCE provisions."[45]

However, in a specific case in which the U.S.S.R. refused a visa for emigration to Israel, it gave a broad definition to family, considering a divorced woman a member of her former husband's family. Her husband had been refused a visa on the grounds of the secret nature of his work. According to the unofficial Helsinki monitoring group in the Soviet Union:

> In January 1976 Maria Slepak received a legal divorce from Vladimir Slepak and applied with her minor son Leonid for reunion with her mother who had suffered two heart attacks, diabetes and other ailments. The refusal of her application was based on the Moscow Visa Office's interpretation of the Final Act: "The Helsinki Accords provide for the unification of families, not their separation. No matter what Soviet courts say, we consider you and Vladimir Slepak one family."[46]

The absence of a definition of family in the Helsinki Final Act thus creates special problems in discerning whether implementation or violation has occurred.

A press report in the *New York Times,* on May 25, 1977, reported the findings of the U.S. State Department regarding the performance of Eastern European countries in permitting their citizens to join family members in the United States. According to the press report,

> the United States has concluded that Bulgaria, Poland, Czechoslovakia and East Germany have performed rather well on family reunification. Bulgaria has settled 22 of 24 cases, Czechoslovakia 13 of 20 cases and East Germany has allowed 40 citizens to join relatives in the United States and has indicated it would give permission to 20 more applicants to leave. The officials were skeptical about the performance of Rumania and the Soviet Union. Yesterday it was reported that the number of Rumanians given permission to join relatives in the United States was considerably below the number in the previous year.[47]

The statistics show that, in this one area, it appears possible to document implementation.

The problem of family reunification arises in the first instance because barriers to emigration, which do not exist in the West, are common in Eastern Europe. Emigration is not considered a right of the citizen in the U.S.S.R., and applications to emigrate have often resulted in deprivation of various sorts. The Helsinki Agreement, unlike the Universal Declaration of Human Rights and the Covenant on Civil and Political Rights, does not recognize a general right to emigrate. The provisions on family reunification have been regarded by some people as specific subclasses of the more general right to emigrate cited in other human rights instruments.[48] Other commentators have feared that the omission from the Helsinki document of the general right to emigrate and the inclusion of only more limited provisions regarding family reunification might result in a watering down of the internationally recognized right to emigrate.[49] Some of the defects in the formulation of the provision on family reunification have been pointed out:

> Regrettably, the Human Contacts section is silent on various other oppressive policies and practices, such as misuse, as by the Soviet Union, of the national security ground for withholding exit visas from its citizens wishing to be reunited with their families, or to travel abroad temporarily; or the requirement of parental permission even for adults, to emigrate; or the total prohibition of emigration of citizens without family abroad—a right guaranteed by Article 12(2) of the Covenant on Civil and Political Rights, to which the Soviet Union is a party.[50]

Following Helsinki, the U.S.S.R. adopted a number of measures which appeared to be efforts to implement the family reunification provisions. They lowered the fee for a Soviet exit visa, determined that the application fee for travel documents need henceforth only be paid if the application was granted, reduced the number of character references required for prospective emigrants, and reduced the review period for rejected applicants from one year to six months.[51]

It has also been reported that the number of Soviet citizens receiving exit visas to join their families in the U.S. increased significantly in the first half of 1976, although the most recent conclusions of the State Department[52] appear to be less optimistic regarding Soviet performance. The increase largely reflected Armenian emigration.

> The number of Jews receiving Soviet exit visas for the United States is only slightly higher than it was before CSCE, and overall Jewish

emigration from the USSR, while up slightly from 1975, is still significantly lower than the peak years of 1972-73. Some prominent Jewish dissidents have, however, been allowed to leave the USSR since the Helsinki summit.[53]

In March, 1977, the U.S. Helsinki Commission held hearings on family reunification. The chairman of the commission, reporting to the House of Representatives on the question of the emigration of Soviet Jews, said:

> The testimony the Commission heard and the research the Commission staff has done indicate that that expectation (emigration for family reunification) while being rewarded in many cases, is being arbitrarily and and capriciously frustrated in many other instances. There has been an unparalleled exodus of some 130,000 Soviet Jews since 1971, and Commission questioning of 630 of those who left the USSR since the Helsinki Accords were signed August 1, 1975, revealed that 76 percent obtained their exit visas within 6 months of applying for them. But in 1975 and 1976 the total number of emigrants each year has been less than half of what it was in 1973, and the National Conference on Soviet Jewry reports that some 180,000 invitations from relatives—55,000 in 1976 alone—have been sent to Jews in the USSR but not yet transformed into successful emigration applications. In fact, the Commission survey found that 40 percent of the successful emigres interviewed had friends or relatives still in the Soviet Union wanting to leave but either refused permission or too intimidated to try for it.[54]

Ethnic German emigration from the U.S.S.R. and Poland to the Federal Republic of Germany has increased sharply since the Helsinki Accord. More than 6,000 Soviet citizens of German descent were granted permission to emigrate to West Germany in the first half of 1976. This increase was attributed by West German diplomats to the Helsinki Accord. The increase from Poland may have resulted, however, from a series of bilateral agreements between Poland and the Federal Republic of Germany rather than from the Helsinki Accord.

Although it is somewhat difficult to draw conclusions from the available statistics, most commentators believe that, in the area of family reunification, some progress is attributable to the provisions of the Helsinki Accord.[55] Although innumerable family separations remain unresolved, this is an area where progress in future implementation gives some cause for hope.

RELIGIOUS LIBERTY—RELIGIOUS CONTACTS

The 35 participating states of the Helsinki Accord hold widely divergent attitudes regarding religious belief, ranging from those of the Holy See to those of the U.S.S.R. Some of the signatory states maintain a rigid separation of church and state, some have "state churches" (a situation which gives particular denominations special privileges in the country), some governments—notably in the Eastern European countries—share a marked hostility towards religious ideology.[56] Even among the latter states, the degree of *de facto* toleration of, or restrictions on, religious freedom diverges widely. Nearly all of the signatory states maintain, in varying degrees, interference in or control of ecclesiastical affairs. Further complicating an evaluation of the degree of religious liberty in a particular state is the dilemma facing both governments and outside observers as to whether a particular form of activity is a legitimate exercise of religious belief or is antistate or subversive activity. In some cases, it is difficult to distinguish religious persecution from political repression.[57]

Efforts to evaluate the implementation of the Helsinki provisions on religious liberty have focused primarily on problems in the Eastern European countries. It is interesting to note, however, that an examination of the implementation of religious liberty in the signatory states has highlighted some basic restrictions on the freedom of churches in Western Europe.

It is evident that the mere adoption of the Helsinki Final Act containing provisions on religious freedom has not changed, and could not be expected to change, the fundamentally hostile attitudes of the Marxist-Leninist states of Eastern Europe towards religious belief.[58] The difficult position of churches and religious believers in Eastern Europe has been extensively documented.[59] The pertinent question is not whether full religious freedom now exists in Eastern Europe—which is obviously not the case—but whether the Helsinki Accord have resulted in any improvement in the inevitable tension between church and state in that area. Principle VII of the Helsinki Final Act provides that:

> The participating States will respect human rights and fundamental
> freedoms, including the freedom of thought, conscience, religion or
> belief, for all without distinction as to race, sex, language or
> religion. . . .Within this framework the participating states will

recognize and respect the freedom of the individual to profess and practise, alone or in community with others, religion or belief acting in accordance with the dictates of his own conscience.

Basket III notes that the participating states "confirm that religious faiths, institutions and organizations practicing within the constitutional framework of the participating States, and their representatives can, in the field of their activities, have contacts and meetings among themselves and exchange information." Some positive steps appear to have been taken in Eastern European countries to implement this provision of Basket III. Such steps may be simply further developments of a process of détente which predates Helsinki. Nevertheless, the Helsinki Accord has been credited by one major religious organization with an improvement in church-state relationships in Eastern Europe. Dwain C. Epps of the World Council of Churches reports that the Helsinki Accord has had an undoubted positive effect on the relationship of the WCC with member churches in Eastern Europe.[60] Since Helsinki, there has been a noticeable relaxation of tension, increased ease in the exchange of visits of church leaders between East and West, and considerably more freedom for church officials to visit parishes in Eastern Europe. The WCC has also noted that it is often more difficult for Eastern Church leaders to obtain visas for Western countries than for Western church leaders to obtain visas for Eastern European countries. The influence of Helsinki has also been evident in improved relations between the churches of East and West Germany.[61]

The WCC has been particularly active in promoting the implementation of the Helsinki Accord. It has printed and circulated about 1,000 copies of the Helsinki Final Act. In itself, this is a significant contribution to implementation since, in the West, the complete text of the Final Act has been difficult to obtain and has not been widely circulated. More significantly, since Helsinki the WCC has organized meetings among churchmen from the East and West. In these meetings, frank discussions on various aspects of religious liberty in all member states have taken place. The WCC also stimulated and promoted the study of human rights and religious liberty in the local churches of Eastern and Western Europe and North America and has collected information on religious liberty in the signatory states. Spokesmen for the WCC stress that this activity has been carried on in the spirit of the Helsinki Accord—defined as an emphasis on positive steps rather than negative criticism, a realization that advancement in human rights is closely linked with disarmament and economic cooperation and the recognition of the importance of economic, social and cultural rights as well as civil and political rights.[62] The experience of the WCC has also illustrated that a great deal can be accomplished for the promotion of human rights—including religious liberty—through patient, quiet efforts aimed at dialogue and mutual understanding.

In 1975, on the occasion of the Fifth General Assembly of the WCC in Nairobi, Father Gleb Yakunin and Lev Regelson, two Soviet dissidents and members of the Russian Orthodox Church, addressed a letter to Dr. Philip Potter, general secretary of the WCC in which they cited a number of restrictions on religious liberty in the Soviet Union and the persecution of Christians as contrary to the Helsinki Final Act. They urged the WCC to become active in the implementation of the Helsinki Accord provisions on religious liberty. Following lengthy debate on the subject at the Nairobi General Assembly, a resolution was adopted requesting the general secretary of the WCC to see to it that the question of religious liberty be the subject of intensive consultations with the member churches in the signatory states of the Helsinki Agreement.

As a follow-up to the Nairobi resolution, the WCC organized (in July 1976) a small private colloquium in Montreux, Switzerland, of 30 people from member churches in the Helsinki signatory states. The colloquium included representatives from Eastern and Western Europe. The following questions directly related to the Helsinki Accord were discussed:

(a) In what way is the Helsinki Declaration being studied in your church?
(b) Can you identify practices in your society which may contradict the spirit or the letter of the Helsinki Declaration?
(c) What possibilities does your church have to aid in the diffusion, study, and understanding of the Helsinki Declaration in your country and in its implementation, particularly with reference to freedom of thought, conscience, religion, or belief?
(d) In what ways does your church envisage further international cooperation amongst the churches in the signatory states for more effective implementation of the Helsinki Declaration?[63]

The WCC provided the participants with a summary of all appeals concerning religious liberty in Eastern Europe received by the council since the Helsinki meeting, as well as a document on restrictions on religious freedom in Western European countries. Studies by private and church-related bodies on the status of religion in Eastern Europe were also provided to participants. While discussing restrictions on religious liberty in Eastern Europe, the participants at the colloquium noted that, in some Western European states, substantial state interference in church affairs had come to be taken for granted by church members. They referred to the necessity for state consent in the appointment of Catholic bishops in some countries (France and Spain), nearly total control of church finances in others (Norway), and certain restrictions on the appointment of pastors. In addition, concern was expressed over the danger that, in countries where state churches with special privileges existed, these privileges might infringe upon the religious freedom of those who belonged to other churches or no church at all. A number of participants from Western Europe and North America referred to other human rights problems in their countries which could be considered contrary to the provisions of the Helsinki Final Accord.

The Montreux colloquium was only one of a series of activities undertaken by the WCC to implement the Helsinki Accord. In March 1977, a small ad hoc planning group (comprising representatives of churches in the U.S.S.R., Romania, Italy, Czechoslovakia, the U.S., the United Kingdom and the German Federal Republic) met at WCC headquarters in Geneva to propose to the churches in the Helsinki area concrete steps for the implementation of human rights and religious liberty in the context of the Final Act. The proposals suggested a common program of studies for churches on human rights and expressed the desire that such studies would be action-oriented, that representatives of churches in various areas would hold meetings to share the results of their studies, that small working groups would be set up to pursue in-depth studies of particular problems on human rights, that specific bodies would be created within each church and national church council to bear responsibility for programs of study and action on human rights and religious liberty and, finally, that an international consultative body would be organized to ensure the implementation of this plan of ecumenical activities. The planning group proposed a second colloquium, to be held in July 1977, in Montreux, to consider the adoption of their proposals and to prepare a document to be presented in an appropriate manner to the full Belgrade Conference in September 1977.[64]

The thoughtful approach of the WCC has been a particularly positive initiative taken to implement the Helsinki Accord. It has involved active participation from representatives of churches in Eastern and Western Europe and has touched upon some of the most delicate human rights problems dividing East and West.

Other organizations and individuals interested in implementation of the Final Act have centered their activities on the circulation of information relating to religious liberty, particularly in Eastern Europe. The U.S. Senate and House of Representatives, in late 1976, voted a resolution urging the U.S.S.R. to grant religious freedom to its citizens and, in particular, to release Georgii Vins from prison. It was widely believed in the West that this leader of the Ukrainian Baptist Church was imprisoned for his religious beliefs.[65]

> In spite of the fact that Georgii Vins was sentenced prior to the Helsinki Conference, his case is one of the most vivid examples of the Soviet government's actions that do not accord with the stipulation of Basket Three of the Helsinki Agreement.[66]

Reportedly, *samizdat* documents on religion that have reached the West "have emphasized the persecution of believers that has taken place since the signing of the Final Act at the Helsinki Conference".[67] Reference has been made to repressive measures taken in the Soviet Union against the Lithuanian Catholic Church, practicing Jews, Pentecostals, Seventh Day Adventists and Eastern Rite Catholics.[68] Andrei Sakharov's letter to President Carter on January 21, 1977, mentioned the persecution of religion in the U.S.S.R., citing especially the situation of Baptists, Pentecostals, members of the True Orthodox Church, and Uniates.

Publications of the U.S.S.R. Helsinki Watch Group have referred to provisions of the Soviet Code on Marriage and the Family, alleged to have been used as a legal justification for taking children away from religious parents. Article 52 of the code provides that "Parents shall educate their children in the spirit of the moral code of the builders of communism." Article 59 provides that "One or both of the parents may be deprived of parental rights where it is estabished that they have . . . exerted a harmful influence on them by their immoral, antisocial behavior." The same sources, however, report that the Helsinki Accord has had an influence in this regard: "Such cases were common from 1971 to 1974, but they have diminished since signing of the Final Act, probably because information on such cases reached the West and provoked a sharp reaction."[69]

The Helsinki Watch Group has also published a document on the right to emigrate for religious reasons:

> The extensive documentation made public by the Helsinki Watch Group . . . details the persecution of hundreds of Pentecostals for religious reasons, persecution which has led whole Pentecostal communities to set up Emigration Councils and to seek the right to emigrate. Pentecostals and other religious believers are subject to arrest, fines for participation in religious rites and discrimination which is written into Soviet law.[70]

The June 1977 report of the U.S. President to the Congressional Helsinki Commission stated that

> Soviet policy on religious contacts not officially approved by the government remained strict during the reporting period, particularly in cases of contact between Soviet and Western Jews . . . . The situation in Eastern Europe concerning religious contacts and availability of information continued to vary considerably. In Poland, Hungary and Romania, for example, Westerners could generally have access to ecclesiastic organizations and individuals with relative ease, while in other countries obstacles were often raised. For the first time in fifteen years, however, Romania, Hungary and Czechoslovakia recently permitted delegates to attend the annual meeting of the European Council of Jewish Communities.[71]

The report contained information on both the refusal to grant visas and the granting of visas in 1976 and 1977 to American Jewish scholars applying to attend cultural and scientific meetings in the Soviet Union. It also referred to two incidents where Americans were detained at the Moscow airport and not allowed entry into the U.S.S.R., apparently for carrying religious items. On the other hand, the report states,

> In a show of tolerance for officially approved religious contacts . . . the Soviet Government announced in April that it was granting per-

mission to a New York interfaith organization to print and ship 10,000 copies of the Pentateuch (the five books of Moses) to the U.S.S.R. as a gift to the Soviet Jewish Community. The agreement came after two years of negotiation with Soviet officials.[72]

The President's report does not refer to questions of religious liberty in countries of Western Europe.

Although the state of religious liberty is certainly not satisfactory in Eastern Europe and continued restrictions on religious liberty exist in Western Europe, some improvement, however slight, has appeared since Helsinki. The initiatives of the WCC, in particular, are encouraging.

FREEDOM OF INFORMATION

Basket III provides that the participating states

make it their aim to facilitate the freer and wider dissemination of information of all kinds, to encourage cooperation in the field of information and the exchange of information with other countries, and to improve the conditions under which journalists from one participating State exercise their profession in another participating State.

In addition, Basket III contains a number of specific provisions concerning the dissemination of oral and printed information and films, cooperation among mass media organizations, and the improvement of working conditions of journalists. Despite these specific provisions, implementation of the Final Act seems to have progressed least in the area of a "freer and wider dissemination of information" between Eastern and Western Europe. The basically divergent ideology among European states regarding freedom of information is undoubtedly responsible for this lack of progress. According to Western conceptions, freedom of information is a fundamental human right from which the state should not derogate except within very narrow limits. Freedom of information should exist across national frontiers, and the danger of propaganda can be countered by permitting the widest possible dissemination of news. Western sources have emphasized the expression "freer . . . dissemination" in the Helsinki Accords. According to the Soviet conception, freedom of information does not exist in the abstract but in a particular socioeconomic context.

Accordingly, information should promote the development of socialism and, thus, the eventual good of the people. Information that is harmful to socialism must be banned. Information is an aspect of state policy and should be controlled by the state.[73]

Clearly, given such varying conceptions, the Eastern and Western signatory states were "either speaking a different language or using the same words to speak of different realities."[74] It is not surprising, therefore, that little progress has been made in implementing the Helsinki provisions on the freer and wider dissemination of information.

Radio Broadcasting

The ideological differences between Eastern and Western Europe have been most evident in the dispute concerning radio broadcasting. Several years ago, the Soviet Union ceased jamming radio broadcasts by the Voice of America and the BBC. However, it continues to jam Radio Free Europe and Radio Liberty, U.S. broadcasting stations based in Western Europe.

No provision of the Helsinki Accords specifically prohibits jamming of radio broadcasts. A U.S. commentator has contended that the prohibition of jamming may be implied from the Final Act despite the absence of a specific prohibition:

> United States negotiators had attempted to insert explicit references to the cessation of jamming. Predictably the effort failed. The Soviet representatives refused to accept precise language and insisted on ambiguous formulas. While declaring its commitment to freedom of information, the Soviet government eluded firm adherence to specific policies. However, in expressing hope for the continued 'expansion in the dissemination of information by radio,' the Final Act implies that jamming of other broadcasts (Radio Liberty, Radio Free Europe, Kol Israel, Radio Peking) should cease.[75]

The U.S.S.R., in its turn, contends that the type of broadcasts made by the jammed stations are, in themselves, violations of the spirit and letter of the Helsinki Accords. In their view, the stations violate détente by broadcasting anti-Soviet propaganda. The Soviet view may be supported by the precise wording of the Final Act:

> The participating States note the expansion in the dissemination of information broadcast by radio and express the hope for the con-

tinuation of this process, so as to meet the interest of mutual understanding among peoples and the aims set forth by this Conference.

It may be argued that "mutual understanding" is not served by the type of material broadcast by the jammed stations. This material often includes information concerning dissidents in Eastern European countries.

> What has particularly irked the Soviet and East European leaders is the Voice of America coverage of news developments regarding human rights and dissident activities in the U.S.S.R. and Eastern Europe. They have construed this coverage. . .as an ideological attack on the Soviet system, interference in their internal affairs and a maneuver to embarrass them at the upcoming Belgrade meeting.[76]

Mr. Erich Mende, member of the Bundestag of the Federal Republic of Germany, has presented the Western position in a report to the Parliamentary Assembly of the Council of Europe:

> It can . . . be argued . . . that the theory, widely, but not universally, held in the east, that state sovereignty should extend over all forms of communication is contrary to the spirit of Helsinki, and that until this attitude changes, RFE/RL will continue to play an irreplaceable role, in that they, unlike national stations, fill an "information vacuum" by supplying impressively researched news and comments on events not of the sender but in the target countries. How else would citizens of Czechoslovakia, for example, learn the actual content of Charter 77, so frequently mentioned by their state-controlled media.[77]

President Carter's recent request to Congress for additional funding for the Voice of America, Radio Free Europe, and Radio Liberty met with hostility from the Soviet Union. The news agency TASS reported on March 24, 1977,

> The report of the U.S. administration quotes the final act of the Helsinki Conference, but the final act does not even contain a hint that would justify the new decision of the U.S. government to mount hostile radio propaganda against the socialist countries. Quite reversely, the act concluded in Helsinki contains clearly-put obligations to abstain from any interference, direct or indirect, individual or collective, in domestic or foreign affairs that are within the internal competence of another participating state.[78]

Clearly, radio broadcasting remains a post-Helsinki bone of contention between Eastern and Western Europe, giving rise to different opinions regarding implementation of the Final Act. The

Belgrade conference has provided an additional opportunity for the East and West to work out their differences on this question in the spirit of détente.

Newspaper Circulation

According to the *Second Semi-Annual Report* of the U.S. President to the congressional Helsinki Commission,

> Availabilty of Western newspapers and periodicals in Warsaw Pact countries remained poor during the reporting period. Only token numbers were imported and sold in selected locations if at all. . . .There was little indication that Eastern governments allowed free access to Western newspapers through institutions such as major public and university libraries which in Western countries often subscribe to Eastern periodicals and newspapers. Nor did most European countries allow free and unhindered mail entry of newspapers paid for by Western relatives or friends.[79]

However, according to reports, publications imported into Poland are available in reading rooms, and the main limitation there on the importation of foreign literature is availability of hard currency.[80]

At the end of 1976, *Le Monde* and *The Times* of London sent only 40 copies of their papers for daily sale to the Soviet Union, and the *International Herald Tribune* sent only 60 copies. Apparently, these copies were intended for foreign visitors and were not readily available to residents. In March 1976, the *Toronto Globe and Mail* began sending 50 copies of its paper daily to Moscow as a result of an order placed by the Soviet Trade Representative in Ottawa. The President's *First Semi-Annual Report* said that one encouraging sign was the willingness of Soviet authorities to permit USIA to distribute 300 copies of its new Russian language intellectual journal *Dialogue* through the mail. It also said that 60,000 copies of the USIA publication *America Illustrated* are distributed on the basis of a bilateral agreement with the U.S.S.R. concluded prior to the Helsinki conference.

Czechoslovakia has reported that, since Helsinki, measures have been taken for increased import of certain selected newspapers and magazines.[81] The U.S.S.R. reported, in February 1977, that "the number of periodical publications from the capitalist countries (apart from Communist parties publications) distributed in the U.S.S.R. has been increased considerably (fivefold)."[82]

Journalists' Working Conditions

The provisions of the Final Act relating to the working conditions of journalists are a specific development of the broader objective in Basket III of facilitating the freer flow of information. These provisions are relatively specific and seem to have been implemented to a certain degree.

One of the provisions of Basket III reads, "The participating States reaffirm that the legitimate pursuit of their professional activity will neither render journalists liable to expulsion nor otherwise penalize them. If an accredited journalist is expelled, he will be informed of the reason for this act and may submit an application for re-examination of his case."

In early 1977, the U.S.S.R. expelled George Krimsky, an American Associated Press correspondent, on the grounds that he engaged in illegal currency operations. It was widely believed in the West that the expulsion occurred because Krimsky reported on the activities of dissidents and not because of his currency transactions. On February 5, 1977, the U.S. State Department announced that the U.S. was expelling a TASS correspondent in retaliation for the expulsion of Krimsky. This once again raises the question referred to above whether retaliation is an appropriate method of implementing the Helsinki Accord. In announcing the expulsion, the State Department said, "We regret this course of action, which is a step backward from the objective of improving working conditions for journalists contained in the Helsinki Final Act and from the more fundamental interest of promoting a freer flow of information."[83] The Director General of TASS, in turn, stated that the U.S. retaliatory action was "at variance with the Final Act of the Conference of Security and Cooperation in Europe."[84] *From Helsinki to Belgrade,* the Interim Report of the U.K. Helsinki Review Group, cites the Helsinki provision on expulsion of journalists in connection with deportation from the U.K. of Agee and Hosenball, two U.S. writers who had published accounts of U.S. C.I.A. activity:

It is significant for the United Kingdom, as well as others, that the Final Act states that an expelled journalist "will be informed of the reason for this act." Even if considerations of security are held to warrant expulsion and although Messrs. Agee and Hosenball were able to bring appeals, it is regrettable that the United Kingdom government offered no detailed reasons for their expulsion.[85]

Other specific situations regarding journalists have led to accusations of violation of the Final Act. In March, 1977, two Jewish dissidents were blocked by KGB agents in Moscow from accompanying Robert Toth, a *Los Angeles Times* reporter, into his apartment for lunch. The reporter claimed that the incident was a violation of the Helsinki provisions on the improvement of working conditions for journalists. He reported the incident to the U.S. Embassy and protested to Soviet authorities.[86] In June 1977, on the eve of his scheduled departure from the U.S.S.R., the same journalist was questioned by Soviet secret police for 12 hours about his contacts with dissidents. The U.S.S.R. Ministry of Foreign Affairs stated that Toth "has been engaged in activities incompatible with the status of a foreign journalist accredited to the U.S.S.R., that is, with the collection of secret information of a political and military character."[87] The *International Herald Tribune* reported on June 17, 1977, that

> The decision to let Mr. Toth leave was made after the U.S. Senate approved a resolution condemning his detention as a "gross violation" of the 1975 Helsinki accords, and after President Carter expressed his "strongest objections" to the Soviet Union.[88]

According to a *New York Times* dispatch of July 12, 1977, TASS, in a seven-page article, called Toth a spy for U.S. agencies and said that, except for Toth, none of the 300 foreign journalists accredited in the U.S.S.R. had lodged any complaints about working conditions in Moscow.[89]

The first report of the President to the U.S. Helsinki Commission in December 1976 details a number of changes for the better that have been made both in the U.S.S.R. for Western journalists and in the U.S. for Eastern European correspondents. The provisions of the Agreement concerning working conditions for journalists provide that improved conditions should be worked out by bilateral arrangements and reciprocity. The U.S. maintains that this is "one of the few Basket Three provisions for which conclusion of a bilateral implementation arrangement after signature of the Final Act was appropriate.''[90] It goes on to cite a number of developments in this area since Helsinki. One of the first implementation steps taken by the U.S.S.R. was the conclusion of bilateral agreements with Western powers on multiple entry-exit visas for journalists. In addition, the U.S.S.R. announced the easing of travel restrictions on journalists. Thereafter, the U.S. announced reciprocal action. The report further cites a number of changes made in the U.S.S.R. to improve working conditions of journalists.

The second report of the President to the Helsinki Commission in June 1977 was less optimistic. It stated,

> Working conditions for journalists in the U.S.S.R. and Eastern Europe generally deteriorated during the reporting period, primarily because of the sensitivity of Communist governments to Western reporting of their human rights violations. The Soviet Union and several Eastern European countries mounted propaganda campaigns accusing the Western press of obstructing CSCE objectives by impeding East-West understanding. The Czechoslovak press, for example, accused Western newsmen of "slinking" around the apartments of dissidents and ignoring the true accomplishments of Czechoslovak workers. Also, American journalists continued to be attacked falsely in the Soviet press for alleged intelligence connections with the clear purpose of trying to restrict their contacts among Soviet citizens.[91]

The report cites a number of specific incidents of harassment of Western journalists in Eastern European countries. It also refers to the arrest in the state of Virginia of a TASS correspondent for repeatedly ignoring a traffic summons "on the incorrect claim that he possessed diplomatic immunity." The Soviet Union called the arrest a violation of the Helsinki Final Act.

The report also states,

> In late March (1977), Czechoslovak officials informed our Embassy that American as well as other Western journalists would no longer receive visas to Czechoslovakia unless they agreed beforehand not to interview Czechoslovak dissidents. We were also told that correspondents whose work Prague considers "objectionable" would not be granted visas. We expressed our concern to the Czechoslovak Government regarding the application of such a policy and emphasized that the policy would work in exactly the opposite direction from the Helsinki CSCE commitment of promoting a freer flow of information and of improving working conditions for journalists.[92]

Positive developments referred to in the report were the opening of a United Press Office in Leningrad in reciprocity for the opening of a TASS office in San Francisco and the sponsoring by Yugoslavia of a conference of some 100 journalists from the Helsinki conference signatory states in Belgrade in April 1977. The journalists discussed the role of the press in implementing the Final Act and the specific provisions on working conditions for journalists.

Contacts Among Journalists

Basket III provides that the participating states "will encourage meetings and contacts both between journalists' organizations and between journalists from the participating States." Relations between journalists from Eastern and Western Europe have been highly influenced by the Cold War. An organization of Western journalists with headquarters in Brussels has a counterpart in an organization of Eastern journalists with headquarters in Prague. Prior to Helsinki, the organizations rarely worked together. Among the results of the Helsinki conference has been the development of clubs of European journalists from both East and West and an improvement in the relations between the two major international organizations of journalists.[93]

During the negotiations at the Helsinki conference, the French delegation proposed that the participating states invite organizations of journalists to create a European Press Club, which would organize periodic meetings of journalists from the participating states. The proposal was rejected because of opposition from Western countries, who were opposed even to the most limited intervention of the government in the domain of journalism. However, following the Helsinki conference, on the initiative of Jean Schwoebel of *Le Monde* and with the initial aid of UNESCO, a European Club of journalists was organized, grouping journalists from 27 signatory states in their individual capacities and popularly known as the Club Schwoebel. Its aim is to provide an opportunity for dialogue, reflection and understanding among journalists of different ideologies and to promote the "spirit of Helsinki." The club has held two meetings thus far in Paris and Yugoslavia and a forthcoming meeting is planned in Strasbourg under the auspices of the Council of

Europe. Papers have been presented and discussed at the meetings on the implementation of the Helsinki Accord and on the circulation of information.

Another club of journalists has been organized under the title the "Club of Capri" (the location of the organizational meeting). It embraces organizations of journalists rather than individual journalists and was founded on the initiative of the National Federation of the Italian Press. Since it groups organizations of journalists belonging to both the major international organizations, it has contributed to a better understanding and collaboration between the international organizations. The Club of Capri, like the Schwoebel Club, was begun expressly as a means of implementing the Helsinki Accord.

COOPERATION IN THE FIELD OF CULTURE

Basket III of the Helsinki Final Act includes a number of provisions relating to increased cultural exchange. The participating states express their intention to expand and improve links in the field of culture through a better circulation of literature, art, and films among the various states. While the Western signatory countries have emphasized other provisions of Basket III, the Eastern European countries have placed great emphasis on these provisions and have found the West wanting.

The Socialist countries claim that they translate more Western books and show more Western films than the West shows about their countries. They claim that, in general, their people are better informed about life in the West than the peoples of the West are about life in Eastern European countries. They contend that there is discrimination against Eastern European films by Western distributors and cite the fact that no Soviet films were shown at the Cannes film festival in 1976.[94]

The comments in the Soviet and East European press relating to cultural exchanges contain numerous references to what are regarded as one-sided exchanges. The deputy minister of culture of the U.S.S.R. has said that "in the Soviet Union there are theatrical performances based on 129 works by Western writers, whereas plays by Soviet writers performed in Western countries can be counted on the fingers of one hand."[95] Following the Helsinki recommendations, the chairman of the U.S.S.R. State

Committee for Television and Radio Broadcasting took steps to increase the exchange of television films by sending 162 Soviet films to 27 television stations in capitalist countries in the first six months of 1976. Apparently the programs were not well received. It was noted that:

Certain circles in the West that control all sources of information including television, are obviously afraid that the working people will learn the truth about the Soviet Union and the achievements of our people. In an effort to discredit socialism, bourgeois propaganda invents all sorts of nonsense about our country and suppresses the real facts by avoiding honest cooperation in the realm of television. This, of course, is completely contrary to the agreements reached in Helsinki, but we are determined to continue our selfless work in the interests of détente.[96]

In the first six months of 1976, the Western "Eurovision" took only 55 programs from the Soviet "Intervision," while "Intervision" took 144 programs from western television in 1975 and 117 in the first half of 1976.

In a speech in 1976, Brezhnev quoted figures indicating that:

the West is very much second to the Socialist countries in its encouragement of cultural and human contacts . . . . For example, in England and France about six or seven times fewer Soviet authors are printed than English and French authors in the Soviet Union. The Western countries show ten times fewer Soviet films than we show Western films, and three times fewer Soviet television programs.[97]

Other complaints of the Soviets are that, even after Helsinki, there are sometimes refusals to supply certain Western publications under the formula "not available for export to iron curtain countries" and that cost of Western publications are prohibitive.

Western commentators agree that, quantitatively, the East's record of publication, translation and showing of films from Western countries is superior to the West's record as regards the East. They attribute this to two factors. First, that Westerners are generally not interested in the cultural material now emanating from the East, which appears often to be mediocre in quality and highly propagandistic. It is claimed that, in general, books and films from the East are simply not competitive on the free market. Secondly, Western commentators point out that importation and translation in the West is carried out by private enterprises over which the state has no direct control. Hence, the state in Western countries cannot simply impose an obligation on publishers to import a certain quantity of material from the East. They also claim that Western material translated and published in Eastern countries has been carefully selected to convey an inaccurate picture of the West to Eastern audiences.[98]

The *Second Semi-Annual Report* of the U.S. President to the Helsinki Commission states: "Though still falling short of fulfilling the resolve expressed in the Final Act to 'increase substantially' cooperation and exchanges, implementation of provisions relating to culture and education continued to be characterized by notable progress."[99]

The President's report calls attention to the evident interest of the Soviet Union and Eastern countries in expanding cultural exchanges and cites an impressive list of recent developments in cultural relations between the U.S. and Eastern European countries, including formal negotations on cultural exchanges with Bulgaria, Czechoslovakia, and Hungary; agreements with Romania and the U.S.S.R., and proposals regarding exchanges with the German Democratic Republic. It also refers to the very positive reaction of the U.S.S.R. to the first agreement for direct exchanges between an American and a Soviet university—the October 1976 agreement between the State University of New York and Moscow State University. It cites increasing activities of the U.S. with Eastern European countries in the fields of publishing, the performing arts, films, and broadcasting.

While referring to these positive developments, the report states:

At the same time, progress in extending relations on the level of direct contacts and communications among persons working in the field of culture and education continues to be hindered in some Eastern countries by fear of ideological contamination. . . Linking dissident activity with exposure to Western bourgeois influences, Soviet and some Eastern European press articles presented increasingly strident warnings of the ideological limits to cooperation, particularly in cultural fields, and hints of a curtailment of further progress in East–West exchanges. This media campaign has shown that the Soviet Union and, to varying degrees, its allies, still adhere to the position advanced by Soviet Deputy Minister for Culture Popov that cooperation and exchanges "without boundaries or barriers" are unacceptable.[100]

Leonard H. Marks, chairman of the U.S. Advisory Commission on International Educational and Cultural Affairs of the Department of State, testified before the Helsinki Commission and expressed disappointment at what he called the Soviet government's "selective policy" of compliance with Basket III provisions. He also referred to Soviet criticism of U.S. compliance:

> Nevertheless, I must admit that, according to Soviet lights, we have given them some grounds for criticism. For example, our refusal to grant entry visas to Soviet trade unionists hardly seems designed to broaden East-West exchange. And it is, I believe, quite true that the private sector has made no unusual effort to encourage the importation of books, films, television programs and the like from Eastern European countries.[101]

Marks went on to make specific suggestions for expanded cultural and educational exchanges, including the establishment of a currency convertibility exchange program and the development of sister city relations between U.S. cities and cities of Eastern Europe. He urged the U.S. to press the Soviet Union to permit the opening of an American bookstore in Moscow, where there would be no control over the selection of books, and referred to the lack of censorship of Russian books entering the U.S.

Some U.S. commentators have criticized what they consider to be inadequate funding of cultural exchange programs by the government. A representative of the U.S. State Department has pointed out that the greatest expansion in cultural exchange since Helsinki has not occurred through government programs but within the private sector, with major funding coming from the American and foreign institutions directly involved.[102]

Eastern Europeans have also criticized the West for failure to emphasize the teaching of Eastern European languages. The teaching of Russian appears to be decreasing in the U.S. The *Interim Report* of the U.K. Helsinki Review Group states that "encouragement to universities to increase, say, language teaching facilities . . . is inherently difficult; it depends in large measure on increasing the interest of students."[103]

The *Report* of the Study Mission to Europe of the U.S. Helsinki

Commission recommended that the commission urge the State Department and appropriate congressional committees to reestablish a program to encourage wider availability of U.S. publications in East Europe by a government guarantee to convert to dollars any soft currencies accepted in payment for U.S. publications. The Association of American Publishers, Inc., subsequently developed an extensive proposal for a currency convertibility plan that could be used as a reference by Congress in drafting legislation. The proposal was specifically labeled a response to Helsinki. It stated,

> In order for the United States to implement a number of the provisions of Basket III of the Accords, the foreign currency barrier must be overcome. Many soft currency countries wish and need our cultural and educational materials. And the U.S. producers of such materials are anxious to make the investments required to effect such sales. However, both sides are frustrated and powerless because of the currency barrier. Hence, this proposal sets forth a plan which will enable such nations to purchase U.S. products in local currency which the American exporter will then exchange for dollars through the U.S. Treasury. The soft currencies thus generated will, in turn, be used to provide programs designed to implement other provisions of the Accords. . . . A new convertibility program is absolutely essential if the U.S. is to implement the cultural and educational exchanges called for in the Helsinki Accords.[104]

This innovative proposal suggests that the soft currency received by the U.S. government under the convertibility system would be spent to implement Helsinki projects in the host country rather than for ongoing U.S. programs such as running the embassy. It suggests, *inter alia,* projects such as training translators and identifying translators who would be able to staff projects designed to bring local books to the attention of U.S. publishers.

> One of the most frequently-voiced complaints of the Eastern European nations is that their books receive very little attention in the West and that the flow of intellectual properties seems to be a one-way street. While there has been some success in the exchange of scientific materials, their complaint is certainly justified insofar as *belles lettres* are concerned."[105]

The proposal terminates with a plea for the adoption of a currency convertibility program as an important means of implementing Basket III.

In exceptionally informative testimony before the Helsinki Commission in May 1977, Robert L. Bernstein, chairman of the Board and president of Random House (a publishing company), referred to a number of problems facing Western publishers of literature from the U.S.S.R.:

1. The unpublished censorship laws of the Soviet Union;
2. The inability of Soviet authors to enter into direct contracts with foreign publishers for publication of their works abroad;
3 Expulsion of Soviet authors from the Writers' Union on account of foreign publication of their work;
4. Extremely difficult telephone and postal communications, particularly with persons considered to be dissidents.

Bernstein said,

> I recommend that securing effective guarantees for the normal delivery of international mail and unimpeded international telephone service should be a high priority for American delegates to the Belgrade Conference. Although there is no explicit mention of telephone and postal communications in the Final Act, such guarantees are obviously essential if we are to realize the human contacts and cultural exchanges called for in that agreement.[106]

Bernstein reported that, as of May 1977, no books published in the West could be purchased by the Soviet public, although Western works translated and published in Russian could be purchased. However, such books were carefully screened for ideological content, and the result was an inaccurate portrayal of Western life. He stated, "It is naive and utopian to believe that we can persuade the Soviet Union to immediately end all censorship, and I would acknowledge their right to ban from sale or circulation in the U.S.S.R. any books that violate provisions of published Soviet laws. But I believe our delegates at Belgrade must make clear that unless ordinary Soviet citizens can have access in some fashion to current Western books beyond those works selected and edited by Communist Party officials for publication inside the U.S.S.R., then cultural exchange and cooperation is a sham and a deception."[107]

He also called attention to certain failings of the U.S. government in its obligations under the Final Act. He stated that the State Department had furnished very little help or guidance to U.S. publishers attempting to increase East-West cultural exchange, even though, by signing the Final Act, the U.S. government had in effect committed private publishers to increase the number of translated books published.

As a result of the Helsinki Final Act and a consensus among its states members, UNESCO undertook several projects intended to carry out activities recommended in the Act, such as setting up a cultural data bank, publishing a detailed annual calendar of cultural events in Europe, and increasing activities by the UNESCO European Centre for Higher Education in Bucharest.[108]

The Inter-Parliamentary Union conducted a detailed inquiry concerning implementation of the Final Act in signatory countries. The replies evidenced increased cultural exchanges following the Helsinki Conference in Canada, Czechoslovakia, Poland, France, the United States, the U.S.S.R., Yugoslavia, the Federal Republic of Germany, and a number of other countries.

Despite the evident divergence in the attitudes of the East and West, it appears that cultural exchange is an area in which the Helsinki Accord has had a certain influence on the action of states. Although such exchanges have been developing since the advent of détente—thus, well before the Helsinki Final Act—the latter seems to have given a new impetus to their development.

CONCLUSIONS

On balance, what can be concluded about the degree of implementation of the human rights and humanitarian provisions of the Final Act two years later? The question raises the perennial problem of whether one perceives the glass as half-empty or half-full. Certainly, the Helsinki Accord has not made fundamental or profound changes in the treatment of nationals in some Eastern European countries. Nor, for that matter, have they resulted in dramatic improvement in human rights problems (such as racial discrimination, unemployment, and political tests for civil servants) in some Western countries. But the expectation that the Accord would have such an effect is basically unrealistic. The humanitarian provisions of Basket III have led to some modest but measurable and positive results. The implementation of the human rights provisions of Principle VII is more difficult to assess, both because of the generality of its provisions and ideological differences between East and West concerning permissible limitations on human rights. Nevertheless, the incorporation of Principle VII in the Final Act has provided an opportunity for dissidents in Eastern European countries to focus world attention on very real problems in their countries; reference to the Final Act in this regard has been more widespread than reference to the binding provisions of the U.N. Covenants on Human Rights, ratified by Eastern European countries.

Thus, these provisions have given legitimacy to discussions concerning human contacts, freedom of information, cultural exchange, and general human rights problems in the context of détente. Unfortunately, these discussions have, thus far, remained largely polemical and have not yet led to a real dialogue concerning divergent conceptions of human rights.

Some seeds have been planted, however, which could lead to a more free exchange of information and contacts between East and West. The initiatives of the WCC and the post-Helsinki clubs of European journalists, as well as proposals for currency convertibility programs, have received almost no publicity in the press, yet they are consequences of the Helsinki conference. Cultural exchanges among signatory nations have also received a new impetus since the Final Act. Popular attention has been focused on accusations of violations of the human rights provisions, but such accusations should not obscure the responsible efforts of the signatory nations to act in the "spirit of Helsinki." As George Kennan has said, in referring to détente, "there is no reason to turn up one's nose at limited improvements just because one cannot have total ones."[109]

Many observers of the post-Helsinki scene have stressed the need for some continuing machinery to assess compliance with the Final Act. Suggestions have ranged from an on-going system for submission of reports and examination of compliance, similar to supervisory machinery provided for in some other human rights treaties, to emphasis on the need for future meetings concerning implementation after Belgrade. There have been suggestions for giving additional recognition to private monitoring groups. All these suggestions reflect a concern that the political will evidenced in the Final Act will not be maintained without a stress on implementation. The political realities of the situation will probably dictate the more limited solution of provision for future meetings on implementation following Belgrade. The Belgrade meeting itself might contribute to future implementation by resolving the impasse over jamming of radio broadcasting and by defining the meaning of "family" under the Accords.

The human rights provisions of the Final Act have also focused attention on the importance of the ratification of the U.N. Covenants on Human Rights. The defects of the human rights provisions of The Final Act are evident—they do not express binding legal commitments, and they are too general. The covenants do not suffer from these defects, and a logical step for countries urging implementation of the human rights provisions of the Helsinki Accord is the ratification of the covenants. In this respect, a number of countries in the West, including the U.S., have been negligent. Among Western signatory nations only Canada, Denmark, West Germany, Norway and the United Kingdom have ratified the covenants. All Eastern European countries and Yugoslavia have ratified them. A more widespread appreciation of the anomaly of this slowness of Western countries in accepting provisions on human rights that are binding and that would compel implementation of the human rights provisions of the Final Act may prove to be one of the greatest contributions of the Helsinki Accord. In an address delivered at Notre Dame, Indiana, in April 1977, A.H. Robertson, formerly of the Council of Europe, stated:

> Seventeen of the thirty-five participants in the Helsinki Conference have ratified the U.N. Covenants on Human Rights. Could one not hope that one result of the follow-up conference in Belgrade should be a recommendation—or, even better, an undertaking—that the other participants should take action to ratify the Covenants, and thus establish reciprocity of obligations about respect for human rights? One would even like to see the establishment of a separate "Human Rights Committee" of the C.S.C.E. States with the task of supervising the application of the human rights provisions of the Helsinki Agreement. . . .Though it would be unrealistic to expect this in the near future, the idea might be retained for the post-Belgrade negotiations.[110]

Although an adequate assessment of compliance with the Final Act will have to await a later date it appears at the present time that the "continuation of the dialogue takes precedence over immediate results."[111] Hence, the relatively modest implementation of the human rights provisions thus far should be no reason for discouragement, nor for breaking the dialogue. The more reasonable outlook would seem to be to consider the glass as half-full rather than half-empty.[112]

NOTES

1. Liskofsky, *Conference on Security and Cooperation in Europe (Helsinki Declaration)*, REPORTS ON THE FOREIGN SCENE 1 (January 1976) at 2-3 (American Jewish Committee, Institute of Human Relations).

2. COMMITTEE ON INTERNATIONAL RELATIONS, U.S. HOUSE OF REPRESENTATIVES, FIRST SEMI-ANNUAL REPORT BY THE PRESIDENT TO THE COMMISSION ON SECURITY AND COOPERATION IN EUROPE 14 (1976) (hereinafter FIRST SEMI-ANNUAL REPORT). This 62-page report contains extensive information on the U.S. view of implementation, up to the date of publication. The remark quoted in the text concerned the U.S. reaction to the way in which the Soviet Union and East European states had interpreted and emphasized certain aspects of the Accord.

3. New York Times, February 24, 1977.

4. 76 DEP'T STATE BULL. 154 (February 21, 1977).

5. 76 DEP'T STATE BULL. 161 (February 28, 1977).

6. FIRST SEMI-ANNUAL REPORT, at ix.

7. New York Times, February 5, 1977.

8. New York Times, March 4, 1977.

9. PARLIAMENTARY ASSEMBLY, COUNCIL OF EUROPE, IMPLEMENTATION OF THE FINAL ACT OF THE CONFERENCE ON SECURITY AND COOPERATION IN EUROPE, AS/Inf (77) 9.

10. Sofinsky, 1977 ZHURNALIST at 71-73; *abstracted in* 29 CURRENT DIG. SOVIET PRESS 5 (No. 10 1977)

11. Strzhizhovsky, Pravda, February 10, 1977, at 5; *condensed in* 29 CURRENT DIG. SOVIET PRESS 5 (No. 6 1977).

12. 29 CURRENT DIG. SOVIET PRESS 5 (No. 6 1977).

13. INTER-PARLIAMENTARY UNION, MEETING OF THE WORKING GROUP ON EUROPEAN COOPERATION AND SECURITY, Europe /77/2 (February 18, 1977) and ACTION TAKEN WITH A VIEW TO IMPLEMENTING THE RECOMMENDATIONS OF THE HELSINKI SUMMIT CONFERENCE, Europe /77/ (February 18, 1977).

14. CHRONICLE OF HUMAN RIGHTS IN THE USSR, July–September, 1976, at 14.

15. New York Times, March 4, 1977.

16. New York Times, April 18, 1977.

17. *To Establish a Commission on Security and Cooperation in Europe: Hearings on H.R. 9466 Before the Subcomm. on International Political and Military Affairs of the House Comm. on International Relations,* 94th Cong., 1st & 2d Sess. 7 (1975-1976) (statement of Representative Millicent Fenwick).

18. *Remarks to the Board of Directors of the International League for Human Rights,* CHRONICLE OF HUMAN RIGHTS IN THE USSR, October–December 1976, at 18.

19. Letter from Robert J. McCloskey (January 19, 1976) *in Id.,* at 4.

20. STUDY MISSION TO EUROPE, REPORT TO THE COMMISSION ON SECURITY AND COOPERATION IN EUROPE 1 (1976).

21. *Id.*

22. Korionov, Pravda, February 17, 1977, at 4; *condensed in* 29 CURRENT DIG. SOVIET PRESS 15 (No. 7 1977).

23. CHRONICLE, October–December 1976, above, note 18, at 15.

24. STUDY MISSION, above, note 20, at 2.

25. *Id.,* at 2-3.

26. HELSINKI REVIEW GROUP, FROM HELSINKI TO BELGRADE: INTERIM REPORT (1977).

27. DOCUMENTS OF THE HELSINKI WATCH GROUP IN THE USSR, vii-viii (No. 1, 1977).

28. *Id.,* at ix and x.

29. Washington Post, February 11, 1977.

30. New York Times, February 12, 1977.

31. 1976 CHRONICLE (No. 22) above, note 14, at 40.

32. Pravda, February 12, 1977, at 4; *reprinted in full in* 29 CURRENT DIG. SOVIET PRESS 2 (No. 6 1977).

33. Charter 77 *reprinted in full* New York Times, January 27, 1977.

34. New York Times, March 17, 1977.

35. Letter from International League for Human Rights to Henry Kissinger (October 1975).

36. SECOND SEMI-ANNUAL REPORT OF THE PRESIDENT TO THE COMMISSION ON SECURITY AND COOPERATION IN EUROPE, DECEMBER 1, 1976–JUNE 1, 1977 39 (mimeographed copy).

37. *Id.,* at 39.

38. Schofield, *La Liberté de Voyage et le Fantôme de McCarthy aux Etats-Unis,* LE MONDE DIPLOMATIQUE, June 1977, at 8.

39. *Id.*

40. New York Times, April 17, 1977.

41. Wall Street Journal, April 18, 1977.

42. FIRST SEMI-ANNUAL REPORT, at 46 (emphasis added).

43. HELSINKI REVIEW GROUP, FROM HELSINKI TO BELGRADE, above, note 26, at 26.

44. *Id.*

45. *Abstract of the Report of the Public Group to Promote Observance of the Helsinki Accords in the USSR, July 22, 1976,* DOCUMENTS OF THE HELSINKI WATCH GROUP IN THE USSR xii (1976).

46. *Id.,* at xvi.

47. New York Times, May 25, 1977.

48. Scrivner, *The Conference on Security and Cooperation in Europe: Implications for Soviet-American Détente,* 6 DENVER J. INT'L L. 139 (1976).

49. Arthur A. Hartman, Assistant U.S. Secretary of State for European Affairs, testified before a Congressional Committee prior to the signing of the Final Act, "I received a delegation from the American Jewish community who were quite concerned that since the area and the specifics of human rights dealt with within these documents might be less comprehensive than the U.N. Declaration on Human Rights, would this in any way be seen as a modification? Well, there are going to be words in here that will make it quite clear that this is not the case." *Hearings Before the Subcomm. of International, Political and Military Affairs of the House Committee on International Relations,* 94th Cong., 1st Sess. 22 (1975).

50. Liskofsky, above, note 1, at 11.

51. FIRST SEMI-ANNUAL REPORT, at 40.

52. New York Times, May 25, 1977.

53. FIRST SEMI-ANNUAL REPORT, at 41.

54. *Speech on HR2367 Before the House of Representatives, March 22, 1977.* 95th Cong., 1st Sess. (1977) (report of Representative Dante Fascell).

55. "Even in the sensitive area of human contacts, such as family reunion, ethnic emigration, and travel in general, the recommendations of Helsinki, combined with Western insistence, public protest, and economic pressure have brought about some success." RADIO FREE EUROPE, RESEARCH REPORT /260 (EASTERN EUROPE), December 23, 1976, at 17.

56. However, the constitutions of the Eastern European socialist countries contain provisions guaranteeing freedom of religious belief.

57. A case in point is that of Georgii Vins in the Soviet Union. This well-known leader of a Baptist group in the Ukraine was sentenced to five years' imprisonment and five years of exile in the Soviet Union in 1975. On January 30, 1975, the officers of the World Council of Churches issued a statement which contained the following comment, "We understand that Mr. Vins is charged with the violation of Soviet law, in particular Article 209-1 of the Ukrainian Criminal Code. We have reason to believe on the basis of information received that the charges against Mr. Vins are made primarily because of his religious convictions and activities."

58. "Despite flexibility of approach in specific circumstances, despite differentiation in ecclesiastical policy from country to country, there can be no doubt that, throughout Eastern Europe, the socialist state conducts an *ideological struggle* against religion. In the pursuit of this struggle, all the resources of the Communist Party—the guiding party of society—and all the organs of state engaged in the construction of a materialist society are mobilized. We are therefore dealing in essence with an ideological process which, even if there is a growing tendency to adopt compromises in practice, can admit of no ultimate concession." G. BARBERINI, CHURCH WITHIN SOCIALISM 13 (E. Weingartner ed. 1976).

59. BARBERINI, CHURCH WITHIN SOCIALISM, above, note 58; CENTRE FOR THE STUDY OF RELIGION AND COMMUNISM, RELIGIOUS LIBERTY IN THE SOVIET UNION: T. BEESON, DISCRETION AND VALOUR, RELIGIOUS CONDITIONS IN RUSSIA AND EASTERN EUROPE (1974).

60. Interview with Dwain C. Epps, staff member, Commission of the Churches on International Affairs, World Council of Churches, in Geneva (June 16, 1977). The WCC is an ecumenical organization of Protestant and Orthodox churches with headquarters in Geneva, Switzerland. The Roman Catholic Church is not a member.

61. *Id.*

62. The concern of the WCC with human rights and the effort to involve local churches in human rights concerns antedates Helsinki. In 1974, an important consultation on "Human Rights and Christian Responsibility" was organized by the WCC in St. Polten, Austria. This consultation provided the orientation for the future work of the WCC in this field, including its work in the implementation of the Helsinki Accord.

63. Human Rights-Post-Assembly Follow-Up, WCC COMMISSION OF THE CHURCHES IN INTERNATIONAL AFFAIRS NEWSLETTER, 1976, No. 4, at 25.

64. Letter from *Ad Hoc* Planning Group, Commission of the Churches on International Affairs, to WCC Member Churches and Associate Councils in the Helsinki Area, March 30, 1977 (WCC, Geneva).

65. *See* above, note 57.

66. Antic, *Anti-Religious Pressures in the U.S.S.R. in the Aftermath of the Helsinki Conference,* RADIO LIBERTY RESEARCH, RL 6/77, January 1, 1977.

67. *Id.*

68. *Id.*

69. DOCUMENTS OF THE HELSINKI WATCH GROUP, above, note 27, at xvii.

70. CHRONICLE OF HUMAN RIGHTS IN THE USSR, January-March, 1977, at 37.

71. SECOND SEMI-ANNUAL REPORT, above, note 36, at 54-56.

72. *Id.*

73. Ghebali, *La Collaboration Transnational entre Journalistes,* LA CIRCULATION DES INFORMATIONS ET LE DROIT INTERNATIONAL (1977).

74. Ghebali, *Les 'mesures de confiance' militaires et le désarmement,* LE MONDE DIPLOMATIQUE, June 1977, at 6.

75. Abshire, *Helsinki and Beyond,* INTERNATIONAL HUMAN RIGHTS 29 (1977).

76. *Hearings Before the Commission on Security and Cooperation in Europe,* 95th, Cong., 1st Sess. 9 (1977) (statement of John E. Reinhardt).

77. *Debate on Implementation of the Final Act of the Conference on Security and Co-operation in Europe,* EUR. CONSULT. ASS. DEB., at 119 (April 27, 28, and 29, 1977).

78. *Hearings Before the Commission,* above, note 76, at 39 (statement of Sig Michelson).

79. SECOND SEMI-ANNUAL REPORT, above, note 36, at 60-61.

80. U.S. Commission on Security and Cooperation in Europe, *Preliminary Staff Report on the Flow of Information Between Helsinki Signatories,* News Release of the CSCE, May 25, 1977.

81. *Meeting of the Working Group on European Co-operation and Security,* Europe /77/2, INTER-PARLIAMENTARY UNION, February 18, 1977, at 23.

82. *The Action Taken with a View to Implementing the Recommendations of the Helsinki Summit Conference and the Belgrade Inter-Parliamentary Conference,* Europe /77/1 INTER-PARLIAMENTARY UNION, February 18, 1977, at 76.

83. 76 DEP'T STATE BULL. (February 28, 1977).

84. LITERATURNAYA GAZETA, February 16, 1977, at 9; *condensed in* 29 CURRENT DIG. SOVIET PRESS 11 (No. 7 1977).

85. HELSINKI REVIEW GROUP, FROM HELSINKI TO BELGRADE, above, note 26, at 28-29.

86. New York Times, March 8, 1977.

87. International Herald Tribune, June 10, 1977.

88. International Herald Tribune, June 17, 1977.

89. New York Times, July 12, 1977.

90. FIRST SEMI-ANNUAL REPORT, at 49.

91. SECOND SEMI-ANNUAL REPORT, above, note 36, at 63-64.

92. *Id.,* at 66.

93. The information for this section of the paper was obtained from an interview with Victor-Yves Ghebali, chargé de recherche, Centre de Recherche sur les Institutions Internationales, in Geneva (June 24, 1977); *also from* Ghebali, *La Collaboration,* above, note 73.

94. FIRST SEMI-ANNUAL REPORT: Szenfeld, *Cooperation in the Field of Cultural Exchanges since the Helsinki Conference,* RADIO LIBERTY RESEARCH RL 7/77 (January 5, 1977).

95. LITERATURNAYA GAZETA, No. 3 (1976); quoted in RADIO LIBERTY RESEARCH, above, note 94, at 2.

96. RADIO LIBERTY RESEARCH, above, note 94, at 9.

97. Moskovskaya pravda, September 3, 1976, at 3; quoted in RADIO LIBERTY RESEARCH, above, note 94, at 9.

98. FIRST SEMI-ANNUAL REPORT, at 52; Sussman, *Let's Not Play the 'Numbers Game' at Belgrade,* FREEDOM AT ISSUE, November-December 1976, at 25.

99. SECOND SEMI-ANNUAL REPORT above, note 36, at 68.

100. *Id.,* at 69-71.

101. *Hearings Before the Commission,* above, note 76, at 60 (statement of Leonard H. Marks).

102. *Hearings Before the Commission,* above, note 76, at 11 (statement of Joseph D. Duffey).

103. HELSINKI REVIEW GROUP, FROM HELSINKI TO BELGRADE, above, note 26, at 29.

104. *Hearings Before the Commission,* above, note 76, at 128-129 (proposal of Leo N. Albert, on behalf of the Association of American Publishers, Inc.).

105. *Id.*

106. *Hearings Before the Commission,* above, note 76, at 6 (testimony of Robert L. Bernstein).

107. *Id.,* at 17.

108. SECOND SEMI-ANNUAL REPORT, above, note 36, at 82.

109. Kennan, *Are All Russians Ten Feet Tall. . . and is the West Blind to the Threat from Within?* FREEDOM AT ISSUE, September-October 1976, at 15.

110. Robertson, *The 'Helsinki Agreement' and Human Rights,* NOTRE DAME UNIVERSITY SYMPOSIUM ON INTERNATIONAL HUMAN RIGHTS AND AMERICAN FOREIGN POLICY (1977).

111. *Debate on Implementation,* above, note 77, at 9.

112. For an excellent evaluation of the interim implementation of the Helsinki Agreement, *see* Ghebali, *Le Bilan Interimaire de la C.S.C.E. a la Veille de Belgrade,* 1977 POLITIQUE ETRANGERE.

APPENDIX

Conference on Security and Co-operation in Europe: Final Act*

[August 1, 1975]

The Conference on Security and Co-operation in Europe, which opened at Helsinki on 3 July 1973 and continued at Geneva from 18 September 1973 to 21 July 1975, was concluded at Helsinki on 1 August 1975 by the High Representatives of Austria, Belgium, Bulgaria, Canada, Cyprus, Czechoslovakia, Denmark, Finland, France, the German Democratic Republic, the Federal Republic of Germany, Greece, the Holy See, Hungary, Iceland, Ireland, Italy, Liechtenstein, Luxembourg, Malta, Monaco, the Netherlands, Norway, Poland, Portugal, Romania, San Marino, Spain, Sweden, Switzerland, Turkey, the Union of Soviet Socialist Republics, the United Kingdom, the United States of America and Yugoslavia.

During the opening and closing stages of the Conference the participants were addressed by the Secretary-General of the United Nations as their guest of honour. The Director-General of UNESCO and the Executive Secretary of the United Nations Economic Commission for Europe addressed the Conference during its second stage.

During the meetings of the second stage of the Conference, contributions were received, and statements heard, from the following non-participating Mediterranean States on various agenda items: the Democratic and Popular Republic of Algeria, the Arab Republic of Egypt, Israel, the Kingdom of Morocco, the Syrian Arab Republic, Tunisia.

Motivated by the political will, in the interest of peoples, to improve and intensify their relations and to contribute in Europe to peace,

* Reproduced from an official text provided by the U.S. Department of State.
[A European conference on security and cooperation was proposed as early as 1954. However, a prerequisite to the success of the Conference, the implementation of the Final Quadripartite Protocol on Berlin, was not completed until June 3, 1972. Multilateral preparatory talks for the Conference began in November 1972. The Conference formally opened in July 1973; the working session began in September 1973 and ended in July 1975, after the preparation of this final document. The document, which was signed by the thirty-five nations participating in the Conference, has no legally binding effect.]

security, justice and co-operation as well as to rapprochement among themselves and with the other States of the world,

Determined, in consequence, to give full effect to the results of the Conference and to assure, among their States and throughout Europe, the benefits deriving from those results and thus to broaden, deepen and make continuing and lasting the process of détente,

The High Representatives of the participating States have solemnly adopted the following:

Questions Relating to Security in Europe

The States participating in the Conference on Security and Co-operation in Europe.,

Reaffirming their objective of promoting better relations among themselves and ensuring conditions in which their people can live in true and lasting peace free from any threat to or attempt against their security;

Convinced of the need to exert efforts to make détente both a continuing and an increasingly viable and comprehensive process, universal in scope, and that the implementation of the results of the Conference on Security and Co-operation in Europe will be a major contribution to this process;

Considering that solidarity among peoples, as well as the common purpose of the participating States in achieving the aims as set forth by the Conference on Security and Co-operation in Europe, should lead to the development of better and closer relations among them in all fields and thus to overcoming the confrontation stemming from the character of their past relations, and to better mutual understanding;

Mindful of their common history and recognizing that the existence of elements common to their traditions and values can assist them in developing their relations, and desiring to search, fully taking into account the individuality and diversity of their positions and views, for possibilities of joining their efforts with a view to overcoming distrust and increasing confidence, solving the problems that separate them and co-operating in the interest of mankind;

Recognizing the indivisibility of security in Europe as well as their common interest in the development of co-operation throughout Europe and among themselves and expressing their intention to pursue efforts accordingly;

Recognizing the close link between peace and security in Europe and in the world as a whole and conscious of the need for each of them to make its contribution to the strengthening of world peace and security and to the promotion of fundamental rights, economic and social progress and well-being for all peoples;

Have adopted the following:

(a) Declaration on Principles Guiding Relations between Participating States

The participating States,

Reaffirming their commitment to peace, security and justice and the continuing development of friendly relations and co-operation;

Recognizing that this commitment, which reflects the interest and aspirations of peoples, constitutes for each participating State a present and future responsibility, heightened by experience of the past;

Reaffirming, in conformity with their membership in the United Nations and in accordance with the purposes and principles of the United Nations, their full and active support for the United Nations and for the enhancement of its role and effectiveness in strengthening international peace, security and justice, and in promoting the solution of international problems, as well as the development of friendly relations and co-operation among States;

Expressing their common adherence to the principles which are set forth below and are in conformity with the Charter of the United Nations, as well as their common will to act, in the application of these principles, in conformity with the purposes and principles of the Charter of the United Nations;

Declare their determination to respect and put into practice, each of them in its relations with all other participating States, irrespective of their political, economic or social systems as well as of their size, geographical location or level of economic development, the following principles, which are all of primary significance, guiding their mutual relations:

I. Sovereign equality, respect for the rights inherent in sovereignty

The participating States will respect each other's sovereign equality and individuality as well as all the rights inherent in and encompassed by its sovereignty, including in particular the right of every State to juridical equality, to territorial integrity and to freedom and political independence. They will also respect each other's right freely to choose and develop its political, social, economic and cultural systems as well as its right to determine its laws and regulations.

Within the framework of international law, all the participating States have equal rights and duties. They will respect each other's right to define and conduct as it wishes its relations with other States in accordance with international law and in the spirit of the present Declaration. They consider that their frontiers can be changed, in accordance with international law, by peaceful means and by agreement. They also have the right to belong or not to belong to international organizations, to be or not to be a party to bilateral or multilateral treaties including the right to be or not to be a party to treaties of alliance; they also have the right to neutrality.

II. Refraining from the threat or use of force

The participating States will refrain in their mutual relations, as well as in their international relations in general, from the threat or use of force against the territorial integrity or political independence of any State, or in any other manner inconsistent with the purposes of the United Nations and with the present Declaration. No consideration may be invoked to serve to warrant resort to the threat or use of force in contravention of this principle.

Accordingly, the participating States will refrain from any acts constituting a threat of force or direct or indirect use of force against another participating State. Likewise they will refrain from any manifestation of force for the purpose of inducing another participating State to renounce the full exercise of its sovereign rights. Likewise they will also refrain in their mutual relations from any act of reprisal by force.

No such threat or use of force will be employed as a means of settling disputes, or questions likely to give rise to disputes, between them.

III. Inviolability of frontiers

The participating States regard as inviolable all one another's frontiers as well as the frontiers of all States in Europe and therefore they will refrain now and in the future from assaulting these frontiers.

Accordingly, they will also refrain from any demand for, or act of, seizure and usurpation of part or all of the territory of any participating State.

IV. Territorial integrity of States

The participating States will respect the territorial integrity of each of the participating States.

Accordingly, they will refrain from any action inconsistent with the purposes and principles of the Charter of the United Nations against the territorial integrity, political independence or the unity of any participating State, and in particular from any such action constituting a threat or use of force.

The participating States will likewise refrain from making each other's territory the object of military occupation or other direct or indirect measures of force in contravention of international law, or the object of acquisition by means of such measures or the threat of them. No such occupation or acquisition will be recognized as legal.

V. Peaceful settlement of disputes

The participating States will settle disputes among them by peaceful means in such a manner as not to endanger international peace and security, and justice.

They will endeavour in good faith and a spirit of co-operation to reach a rapid and equitable solution on the basis of international law.

For this purpose they will use such means as negotiation, enquiry, mediation, conciliation, arbitration, judicial settlement or other peaceful means of their own choice including any settlement procedure agreed to in advance of disputes to which they are parties.

In the event of failure to reach a solution by any of the above peaceful means, the parties to a dispute will continue to seek a mutually agreed way to settle the dispute peacefully.

Participating States, parties to a dispute among them, as well as other participating States, will refrain from any action which might aggravate the situation to such a degree as to endanger the maintenance of international peace and security and thereby make a peaceful settlement of the dispute more difficult.

VI. Non-intervention in internal affairs

The participating States will refrain from any intervention, direct or indirect, individual or collective, in the internal or external affairs falling within the domestic jurisdiction of another participating State, regardless of their mutual relations.

They will accordingly refrain from any form of armed intervention or threat of such intervention against another participating State.

They will likewise in all circumstances refrain from any other act of military, or of political, economic or other coercion designed to subordinate to their own interest the exercise by another participating State of the rights inherent in its sovereignty and thus to secure advantage of any kind.

Accordingly, they will, inter alia, refrain from direct or indirect assistance to terrorist activities, or to subversive or other activities directed towards the violent overthrow of the regime of another participating State.

VII. Respect for human rights and fundamental freedoms, including the freedom of thought, conscience, religion or belief

The participating States will respect human rights and fundamental freedoms, including the freedom of thought, conscience, religion or belief, for all without distinction as to race, sex, language or religion.

They will promote and encourage the effective exercise of civil, political, economic, social, cultural and other rights and freedoms all of which derive from the inherent dignity of the human person and are essential for his free and full development.

Within this framework the participating States will recognize and respect the freedom of the individual to profess and practise, alone or in community with others, religion or belief acting in accordance with the dictates of his own conscience.

The participating States on whose territory national minorities exist will respect the right of persons belonging to such minorities to equality before the law, will afford them the full opportunity for the actual enjoyment of human rights and fundamental freedoms and will, in this manner, protect their legitimate interests in this sphere.

The participating States recognize the universal significance of human rights and fundamental freedoms, respect for which is an essential factor for the peace, justice and well-being necessary to ensure the development of friendly relations and co-operation among themselves as among all States.

They will constantly respect these rights and freedoms in their mutual relations and will endeavour jointly and separately, including in co-operation with the United Nations, to promote universal and effective respect for them.

They confirm the right of the individual to know and act upon his rights and duties in this field.

In the field of human rights and fundamental freedoms, the participating States will act in conformity with the purposes and principles of the Charter of the United Nations and with the Universal Declaration of Human Rights. They will also fulfill their obligations as set forth in the international declarations and agreements in this field, including inter alia the International Covenants on Human Rights, by which they may be bound.

VIII. Equal rights and self-determination of peoples

The participating States will respect the equal rights of peoples and their right to self-determination, acting at all times in conformity with the purposes and principles of the Charter of the United Nations and with the relevant norms of international law, including those relating to territorial integrity of States.

By virtue of the principle of equal rights and self-determination of peoples, all peoples always have the right, in full freedom, to determine, when and as they wish, their internal and external political status, without external interference, and to pursue as they wish their political, economic, social and cultural development.

The participating States reaffirm the universal significance of respect for an effective exercise of equal rights and self-determination of peoples for the development of friendly relations among themselves or among all States; they also recall the importance of the elimination of any form of violation of this principle.

IX. Co-operation among States

The participating States will develop their co-operation with one another and with all States in all fields in accordance with the purposes and principles of the Charter of the United Nations. In developing their co-operation the participating States will place special emphasis on the fields as set forth within the framework of the Conference on Security and Co-operation in Europe, with each of them making its contribution in conditions of full equality.

They will endeavour, in developing their co-operation as equals, to promote mutual understanding and confidence, friendly and good-neighbourly relations among themselves, international peace, security and justice. They will equally endeavour, in developing their co-operation, to improve the well-being of peoples and contribute to the fulfilment of their aspirations through, inter alia, the benefits resulting from increased mutual knowledge and from progress and achievement in the economic, scientific, technological, social, cultural and humanitarian fields. They will take steps to promote conditions favourable to making these benefits available to all; they will take into account the interest of all in the narrowing of differences in the levels of economic development, and in particular the interest of developing countries throughout the world.

They confirm that governments, institutions, organizations and persons have a relevant and positive role to play in contributing toward the achievement of these aims of their co-operation.

They will strive, in increasing their co-operation as set forth above, to develop closer relations among themselves on an improved and more enduring basis for the benefit of peoples.

X. Fulfilment in good faith of obligations under international law

The participating States will fulfil in good faith their obligations under international law, both those obligations arising from the generally recognized principles and rules of international law and those obligations arising from treaties or other agreements, in conformity with international law, to which they are parties.

In exercising their sovereign rights, including the right to determine their laws and regulations, they will conform with their legal obligations under international law; they will furthermore pay due regard to and implement the provisions in the Final Act of the Conference on Security and Co-operation in Europe.

The participating States confirm that in the event of a conflict between the obligations of the members of the United Nations under the Charter of the United Nations and their obligations under any treaty or other international agreement, their obligations under the Charter will prevail, in accordance with Article 103 of the Charter of the United Nations.

All the principles set forth above are of primary significance and, accordingly, they will be equally and unreservedly applied, each of them being interpreted taking into account the others.

The participating States express their determination fully to respect and apply these principles, as set forth in the present Declaration, in all aspects, to their mutual relations and co-operation in order to ensure to each participating State the benefits resulting from the respect and application of these principles by all.

The participating States, paying due regard to the principles above and, in particular, to the first sentence of the tenth principle. "Fulfillment in good faith of obligations under international law", note that the present Declaration does not affect their rights and obligations, nor the corresponding treaties and other agreements and arrangements.

The participating States express the conviction that respect for these principles will encourage the development of normal and friendly relations and the progress of co-operation among them in all fields. They also express the conviction that respect for these principles will encourage the development of political contacts among them which in turn would contribute to better mutual understanding of their positions and views.

The participating States declare their intention to conduct their relations with all other States in the spirit of the principles contained in the present Declaration.

(b) Matters related to giving effect to certain of the above Principles

The participating States,

Reaffirming that they will respect and give effect to refraining from the threat or use of force and convinced of the necessity to make it an effective norm of international life,

Declare that they are resolved to respect and carry out, in their relations with one another, inter alia, the following provisions which are in conformity with the Declaration on Principles Guiding Relations between Participating States:

— To give effect and expression, by all the ways and forms which they consider appropriate, to the duty to refrain from the threat or use of force in their relations with one another.

— To refrain from any use of armed forces inconsistent with the purposes and principles of the Charter of the United Nations and the provisions of the Declaration on Principles Guiding Relations between Participating States, against another participating State, in particular from invasion of or attack on its territory.

— To refrain from any manifestation of force for the purpose of inducing another participating State to renounce the full exercise of its sovereign rights.

— To refrain from any act of economic coercion designed to subordinate to their own interest the exercise by another participating State of the rights inherent in its sovereignty and thus to secure advantages of any kind.

— To take effective measures which by their scope and by their nature constitute steps towards the ultimate achievement of general and complete disarmament under strict and effective international control.

— To promote, by all means which each of them considers appropriate, a climate of confidence and respect among peoples consonant with their duty to refrain from propaganda for wars of aggression or for any threat or use of force inconsistent with the purposes of the United Nations and with the Declaration on Principles Guiding Relations between Participating States, against another participating State.

— To make every effort to settle exclusively by peaceful means any dispute between them, the continuance of which is likely to endanger the maintenance of international peace and security in Europe, and to seek, first of all, a solution through the peaceful means set forth in Article 33 of the United Nations Charter.
To refrain from any action which could hinder the peaceful settlement of disputes between the participating States.

The participating States,

Reaffirming their determination to settle their disputes as set forth in the Principle of Peaceful Settlement of Disputes;

Convinced that the peaceful settlement of disputes is a complement to refraining from the threat or use of force, both being essential though not exclusive factors for the maintenance and consolidation of peace and security;

Desiring to reinforce and to improve the methods at their disposal for the peaceful settlement of disputes;

1. Are resolved to pursue the examination and elaboration of a generally acceptable method for the peaceful settlement of disputes aimed at complementing existing methods, and to continue to this end to work upon the "Draft Convention on a European System for the Peaceful Settlement of Disputes" submitted by Switzerland during the second stage of the Conference on Security and Co-operation in Europe, as well as other proposals relating to it and directed towards the elaboration of such a method.

2. Decide that, on the invitation of Switzerland, a meeting of experts of all the participating States will be convoked in order to fulfil the mandate described in paragraph 1 above within the framework and under the procedures of the follow-up to the Conference laid down in the chapter "Follow-up to the Conference".

3. This meeting of experts will take place after the meeting of the representatives appointed by the Ministers of Foreign Affairs of the participating States, scheduled according to the chapter "Follow-up to the Conference" for 1977; the results of the work of this meeting of experts will be submitted to Governments.

• • •

Co-operation in Humanitarian and Other Fields

The participating States,

Desiring to contribute to the strengthening of peace and understanding among peoples and to the spiritual enrichment of the human personality without distinction as to race, sex, language or religion,

Conscious that increased cultural and educational exchanges, broader dissemination of information, contacts between people, and the solution of humanitarian problems will contribute to the attainment of these aims,

Determined therefore to co-operate among themselves, irrespective of their political, economic and social systems, in order to create better conditions in the above fields, to develop and strengthen existing forms of co-operation and to work out new ways and means appropriate to these aims,

Convinced that this co-operation should take place in full respect for the principles guiding relations among participating States as set forth in the relevant document,

Have adopted the following:

1. Human Contacts

The participating States,

Considering the development of contacts to be an important element in the strengthening of friendly relations and trust among peoples,

Affirming, in relation to their present effort to improve conditions in this area, the importance they attach to humanitarian considerations,

Desiring in this spirit to develop, with the continuance of détente, further efforts to achieve continuing progress in this field

And conscious that the questions relevant hereto must be settled by the States concerned under mutually acceptable conditions,

Make it their aim to facilitate freer movement and contacts, individually and collectively, whether privately or officially, among persons, institutions and organizations of the participating States, and to contribute to the solution of the humanitarian problems that arise in that connexion,

Declare their readiness to these ends to take measures which they consider appropriate and to conclude agreements or arrangements among themselves, as may be needed, and

Express their intention now to proceed to the implementation of the following:

(a) Contacts and Regular Meetings on the Basis of Family Ties

In order to promote further development of contacts on the basis of family ties the participating States will favourably consider applications for travel with the purpose of allowing persons to enter or leave their territory temporarily, and on a regular basis if desired, in order to visit members of their families.

Applications for temporary visits to meet members of their families will be dealt with without distinction as to the country of origin or destination: existing requirements for travel documents and visas will be applied in this spirit. The preparation and issue of such documents and visas will be effected within reasonable time limits: cases of urgent necessity — such as serious illness or death -- will be given priority treatment. They will take such steps as may be necessary to ensure that the fees for official travel documents and visas are acceptable.

They confirm that the presentation of an application concerning contacts on the basis of family ties will not modify the rights and obligations of the applicant or of members of his family.

(b) Reunification of Families

The participating States will deal in a positive and humanitarian spirit with the applications of persons who wish to be reunited with members of their family, with special attention being given to requests of an urgent character — such as requests submitted by persons who are ill or old.

They will deal with applications in this field as expeditiously as possible.

They will lower where necessary the fees charged in connexion with these applications to ensure that they are at a moderate level.

Applications for the purpose of family reunification which are not granted may be renewed at the appropriate level and will be reconsidered at reasonably short intervals by the authorities of the country of residence or destination, whichever is concerned; under such circumstances fees will be charged only when applications are granted.

Persons whose applications for family reunification are granted may bring with them or ship their household and personal effects; to this end the participating States will use all possibilities provided by existing regulations.

Until members of the same family are reunited meetings and contacts between them may take place in accordance with the modalities for contacts on the basis of family ties.

The participating States will support the efforts of Red Cross and Red Crescent Societies concerned with the problems of family reunification.

They confirm that the presentation of an application concerning family reunification will not modify the rights and obligations of the applicant or of members of his family.

The receiving participating State will take appropriate care with regard to employment for persons from other participating States who take up permanent residence in that State in connexion with family reunification with its citizens and see that they are afforded opportunities equal to those enjoyed by its own citizens for education, medical assistance and social security.

(c) Marriage between Citizens of Different States

The participating States will examine favourably and on the basis of humanitarian considerations requests for exit or entry permits from persons who have decided to marry a citizen from another participating State.

The processing and issuing of the documents required for the above purposes and for the marriage will be in accordance with the provisions accepted for family reunification.

In dealing with requests from couples from different participating States, once married, to enable them and the minor children of their marriage to transfer their permanent residence to a State in which either one is normally a resident, the participating States will also apply the provisions accepted for family reunification.

(d) Travel for Personal or Professional Reasons

The participating States intend to facilitate wider travel by their citizens for personal or professional reasons and to this end they intend in particular:

—gradually to simplify and to administer flexibly the procedures for exit and entry;

—to ease regulations concerning movement of citizens from the other participating States in their territory, with due regard to security requirements.

They will endeavour gradually to lower, where necessary, the fees for visas and official travel documents.

They intend to consider, as necessary, means—including, in so far as appropriate, the conclusion of multilateral or bilateral consular conventions or other relevant agreements or understandings—for the improvement of arrangements to provide consular services, including legal and consular assistance.

* * *

They confirm that religious faiths, institutions and organizations, practising within the constitutional framework of the participating States, and their representatives can, in the field of their activities, have contacts and meetings among themselves and exchange information.

(e) Improvement of Conditions for Tourism on an Individual or Collective Basis

The participating States consider that tourism contributes to a fuller knowledge of the life, culture and history of other countries, to the growth of understanding among peoples, to the improvement of contacts and to the broader use of leisure. They intend to promote the development of tourism, on an individual or collective basis, and, in particular, they intend:

—to promote visits to their respective countries by encouraging the provision of appropriate facilities and the simplification and expediting of necessary formalities relating to such visits;

—to increase, on the basis of appropriate agreements or arrangements where necessary, co-operation in the development of tourism, in particular by considering bilaterally possible ways to increase information relating to travel to other countries and to the reception and service of tourists, and other related questions of mutual interest.

(f) Meetings among Young People

The participating States intend to further the development of contacts and exchanges among young people by encouraging:

—increased exchanges and contacts on a short or long term basis among young people working, training or undergoing education through bilateral or multilateral agreements or regular programmes in all cases where it is possible;

—study by their youth organizations of the question of possible agreements relating to frameworks of multilateral youth co-operation;

—agreements or regular programmes relating to the organization of exchanges of students, of international youth seminars, of courses of professional training and foreign language study;

—the further development of youth tourism and the provision to this end of appropriate facilities;

—the development, where possible, of exchanges, contacts and co-operation on a bilateral or multilateral basis between their organizations which represent wide circles of young people working, training or undergoing education;

—awareness among youth of the importance of developing mutual understanding and of strengthening friendly relations and confidence among peoples.

(g) Sport

In order to expand existing links and co-operation in the field of sport the participating States will encourage contacts and exchanges of this kind, including sports meetings and competitions of all sorts, on the basis of the established international rules, regulations and practice.

(h) Expansion of Contacts

By way of further developing contacts among governmental institutions and non-governmental organizations and associations, including women's organizations, the participating States will facilitate the convening of meetings as well as travel by delegations, groups and individuals.

2. Information

The participating States,

Conscious of the need for an ever wider knowledge and understanding of the various aspects of life in other participating States,

Acknowledging the contribution of this process to the growth of confidence between peoples,

Desiring, with the development of mutual understanding between the participating States and with the further improvement of their relations, to continue further efforts towards progress in this field,

Recognizing the importance of the dissemination of information from the other participating States and of a better acquaintance with such information,

Emphasizing therefore the essential and influential role of the press, radio, television, cinema and news agencies and of the journalists working in these fields,

Make it their aim to facilitate the freer and wider dissemination of information of all kinds, to encourage co-operation in the field of information and the exchange of information with other countries, and to improve the conditions under which journalists from one participating State exercise their profession in another participating State, and

Express their intention in particular:

(a) Improvement of the Circulation of, Access to, and Exchange of Information

(i) *Oral Information*

—To facilitate the dissemination of oral information through the encouragement of lectures and lecture tours by personalities and specialists from the other participating States, as well as exchanges of opinions at round table meetings, seminars, symposia, summer schools, congresses and other bilateral and multilateral meetings.

(ii) *Printed Information*

—To facilitate the improvement of the dissemination, on their territory, of newspapers and printed publications, periodical and non-periodical, from the other participating States. For this purpose:

they will encourage their competent firms and organizations to conclude agreements and contracts designed gradually to increase the quantities and the number of titles of newspapers and publications imported from the other participating States. These agreements and contracts should in particular mention the speediest conditions of delivery and the use of the normal channels existing in each country for the distribution of its own publications and newspapers, as well as forms and means of payment agreed between the parties making it possible to achieve the objectives aimed at by these agreements and contracts;

where necessary, they will take appropriate measures to achieve the above objectives and to implement the provisions contained in the agreements and contracts.

—To contribute to the improvement of access by the public to periodical and non-periodical printed publications imported on the bases indicated above. In particular:

they will encourage an increase in the number of places where these publications are on sale;

they will facilitate the availability of these periodical publications during congresses, conferences, official visits and other international events and to tourists during the season;

they will develop the possibilities for taking out subscriptions according to the modalities particular to each country;

they will improve the opportunities for reading and borrowing these publications in large public libraries and their reading rooms as well as in university libraries.

They intend to improve the possibilities for acquaintance with bulletins of official information issued by diplomatic missions and distributed by those missions on the basis of arrangements acceptable to the interested parties.

(iii) *Filmed and Broadcast Information*

—To promote the improvement of the dissemination of filmed and broadcast information. To this end:

they will encourage the wider showing and broadcasting of a greater variety of recorded and filmed information from the other participating States, illustrating the various aspects of life in their countries and received on the basis of such agreements or arrangements as may be necessary between the organizations and firms directly concerned;

they will facilitate the import by competent organizations and firms of recorded audio-visual material from the other participating States.

The participating States note the expansion in the dissemination of information broadcast by radio, and express the hope for the continuation of this process, so as to meet the interest of mutual understanding among peoples and the aims set forth by this Conference.

(b) Co-operation in the Field of Information

—To encourage co-operation in the field of information on the basis of short or long term agreements or arrangements. In particular:

they will favour increased co-operation among mass media organizations, including press agencies, as well as among publishing houses and organizations;

they will favour co-operation among public or private, national or international radio and television organizations, in particular through the exchange of both live and recorded radio and television programmes, and through the joint production and the broadcasting and distribution of such programmes;

they will encourage meetings and contacts both between journalists' organizations and between journalists from the participating States;

they will view favourably the possibilities of arrangements between periodical publications as well as between newspapers from the participating States, for the purpose of exchanging and publishing articles;

they will encourage the exchange of technical information as well as the organization of joint research and meetings devoted to the exchange of experience and views between experts in the field of the press, radio and television.

(c) Improvement of Working Conditions for Journalists

The participating States, desiring to improve the conditions under which journalists from one participating State exercise their profession in another participating State, intend in particular to:

—examine in a favourable spirit and within a suitable and reasonable time scale requests from journalists for visas;

—grant to permanently accredited journalists of the participating States, on the basis of arrangements, multiple entry and exit visas for specified periods;

—facilitate the issue to accredited journalists of the participating States of permits for stay in their country of temporary residence and, if and when these are necessary, of other official papers which it is appropriate for them to have;

—ease, on a basis of reciprocity, procedures for arranging travel by journalists of the participating States in the country where they are exercising their profession, and to provide progressively greater opportunities for such travel, subject to the observance of regulations relating to the existence of areas closed for security reasons;

—ensure that requests by such journalists for such travel receive, in so far as possible, an expeditious response, taking into account the time scale of the request;

—increase the opportunities for journalists of the participating States to communicate personally with their sources, including organizations and official institutions;

—grant to journalists of the participating States the right to import, subject only to its being taken out again, the technical equipment (photographic, cinematographic, tape recorder, radio and television) necessary for the exercise of their profession;*

—enable journalists of the other participating States, whether permanently or temporarily accredited, to transmit completely, normally and rapidly by means recognized by the participating States to the information organs which they represent, the results of their professional activity, including tape recordings and undeveloped film, for the purpose of publication or of broadcasting on the radio or television.

---

* While recognizing that appropriate local personnel are employed by foreign journalists in many instances, the participating States note that the above provisions would be applied, subject to the observance of the appropriate rules, to persons from the other participating States, who are regularly and professionally engaged as technicians, photographers or cameramen of the press, radio, television or cinema.

The participating States reaffirm that the legitimate pursuit of their professional activity will neither render journalists liable to expulsion nor otherwise penalize them. If an accredited journalist is expelled, he will be informed of the reasons for this act and may submit an application for re-examination of his case.

3. Co-operation and Exchanges in the Field of Culture

The participating States,

Considering that cultural exchanges and co-operation contribute to a better comprehension among people and among peoples, and thus promote a lasting understanding among States,

Confirming the conclusions already formulated in this field at the multilateral level, particularly at the Intergovernmental Conference on Cultural Policies in Europe, organized by UNESCO in Helsinki in June 1972, where interest was manifested in the active participation of the broadest possible social groups in an increasingly diversified cultural life,

Desiring, with the development of mutual confidence and the further improvement of relations between the participating States, to continue further efforts toward progress in this field,

Disposed in this spirit to increase substantially their cultural exchanges, with regard both to persons and to cultural works, and to develop among them an active co-operation, both at the bilateral and the multilateral level, in all the fields of culture,

Convinced that such a development of their mutual relations will contribute to the enrichment of the respective cultures, while respecting the originality of each, as well as to the reinforcement among them of a consciousness of common values, while continuing to develop cultural co-operation with other countries of the world,

Declare that they jointly set themselves the following objectives:

(a)   to develop the mutual exchange of information with a view to a better knowledge of respective cultural achievements,

(b)   to improve the facilities for the exchange and for the dissemination of cultural property,

(c)   to promote access by all to respective cultural achievements,

(d)   to develop contacts and co-operation among persons active in the field of culture,

(e)   to seek new fields and forms of cultural co-operation,

Thus *give expression to* their common will to take progressive, coherent and long-term action in order to achieve the objectives of the present declaration; and

Express their intention now to proceed to the implementation of the following:

Extension of Relations

To expand, and improve at the various levels co-operation and links in the field of culture, in particular by:

—concluding, where appropriate, agreements on a bilateral or multilateral basis, providing for the extension of relations among competent State institutions and non-governmental organizations in the field of culture, as well as among people engaged in cultural activities, taking into account the need both for flexibility and the fullest possible use of existing agreements, and bearing in mind that agreements and also other arrangements constitute important means of developing cultural co-operation and exchanges;

—contributing to the development of direct communication and co-operation among relevant State institutions and non-governmental organizations, including, where necessary, such communication and co-operation carried out on the basis of special agreements and arrangements;

—encouraging direct contacts and communications among persons engaged in cultural activities, including, where necessary, such contacts and communications carried out on the basis of special agreements and arrangements.

Mutual Knowledge

Within their competence to adopt, on a bilateral and multilateral level, appropriate measures which would give their peoples a more comprehensive and complete mutual knowledge of their achievements in the various fields of culture, and among them:

—to examine jointly, if necessary with the assistance of appropriate international organizations, the possible creation in Europe and the structure of a bank of cultural data, which would collect information from the participating countries and make it available to its correspondents on their request, and to convene for this purpose a meeting of experts from interested States;

—to consider, if necessary in conjunction with appropriate international organizations, ways of compiling in Europe an inventory of documentary films of a cultural or scientific nature from the participating States;

—to encourage more frequent book exhibitions and to examine the possibility of organizing periodically in Europe a large-scale exhibition of books from the participating States;

—to promote the systematic exchange, between the institutions concerned and publishing houses, of catalogues of available books as well as of pre-publication material which will include, as far as possible, all, forthcoming publications; and also to promote the exchange of material between firms publishing encyclopaedias, with a view to improving the presentation of each country;

—to examine jointly questions of expanding and improving exchanges of information in the various fields of culture, such as theatre, music, library work as well as the conservation and restoration of cultural property.

Exchanges and Dissemination

To contribute to the improvement of facilities for exchanges and the dissemination of cultural property, by appropriate means, in particular by:

—studying the possibilities for harmonizing and reducing the charges relating to international commercial exchanges of books and other cultural materials, and also for new means of insuring works of art in foreign exhibitions and for reducing the risks of damage or loss to which these works are exposed by their movement;

—facilitating the formalities of customs clearance, in good time for programmes of artistic events, of the works of art, materials and accessories appearing on lists agreed upon by the organizers of these events;

—encouraging meetings among representatives of competent organizations and relevant firms to examine measures within their field of activity—such as the simplification of orders, time limits for sending supplies and modalities of payment—which might facilitate international commercial exchanges of books;

—promoting the loan and exchange of films among their film institutes and film libraries;

—encouraging the exchange of information among interested parties concerning events of a cultural character foreseen in the participating States, in fields where this is most appropriate, such as music, theatre and the plastic and graphic arts, with a view to contributing to the compilation and publication of a calendar of such events, with the assistance, where necessary, of the appropriate international organizations;

—encouraging a study of the impact which the foreseeable development, and a possible harmonization among interested parties, of the technical means used for the dissemination of culture might have on the development of cultural co-operation and exchanges, while keeping in view the preservation of the diversity and originality of their respective cultures;

—encouraging, in the way they deem appropriate, within their cultural policies, the further development of interest in the cultural heritage of the other participating States, conscious of the merits and the value of each culture;

—endeavouring to ensure the full and effective application of the international agreements and conventions on copyrights and on circulation of cultural property to which they are party or to which they may decide in the future to become party.

Access

To promote fuller mutual access by all to the achievements—works, experiences and performing arts—in the various fields of culture of their countries, and to that end to make the best possible efforts, in accordance with their competence, more particularly:

—to promote wider dissemination of books and artistic works, in particular by such means as:

facilitating, while taking full account of the international copyright conventions to which they are party, international contacts and recommendations between authors and publishing houses as well as other cultural institutions, with a view to a more complete mutual access to cultural achievements;

recommending that, in determining the size of editions, publishing houses take into account also the demand from the other participating States, and that rights of sale in other participating States be granted, where possible, to several sales organizations of the importing countries, by agreement between interested partners;

encouraging competent organizations and relevant firms to conclude agreements and contracts and contributing, by this means, to a gradual increase in the number and diversity of works by authors from the other participating States available in the original and in translation in their libraries and bookshops;

promoting, where deemed appropriate, an increase in the number of sales outlets where books by authors from the other participating States, imported in the original on the basis of agreements and contracts, and in translation, are for sale;

promoting, on a wider scale, the translation of works in the sphere of literature and other fields of cultural activity, produced in the languages of the other participating States, especially from the less widely-spoken languages, and the publication and dissemination of the translated works by such measures as:

encouraging more regular contacts between interested publishing houses;

developing their efforts in the basic and advanced training of translators;

encouraging, by appropriate means, the publishing houses of their countries to publish translations;

facilitating the exchange between publishers and interested institutions of lists of books which might be translated;

promoting between their countries the professional activity and cooperation of translators;

carrying out joint studies on ways of further promoting translations and their dissemination;

improving and expanding exchanges of books, bibliographies and catalogue cards between libraries;

—to envisage other appropriate measures which would permit, where necessary by mutual agreement among interested parties, the facilitation of access to their respective cultural achievements, in particular in the field of books;

—to contribute by appropriate means to the wider use of the mass media in order to improve mutual acquaintance with the cultural life of each;

—to seek to develop the necessary conditions for migrant workers and their families to preserve their links with their national culture, and also to adapt themselves to their new cultural environment;

—to encourage the competent bodies and enterprises to make a wider choice and effect wider distribution of full-length and documentary films from the other participating States, and to promote more frequent non-commercial showings, such as premières, film weeks and festivals, giving due consideration to films from countries whose cinematographic works are less well known;

—to promote, by appropriate means, the extension of opportunities for specialists from the other participating States to work with materials of a cultural character from film and audio-visual archives, within the framework of the existing rules for work on such archival materials;

—to encourage a joint study by interested bodies, where appropriate with the assistance of the competent international organizations, of the expediency and the conditions for the establishment of a repertory of their recorded television programmes of a cultural nature, as well as of the means of viewing them rapidly in order to facilitate their selection and possible acquisition.

Contacts and Co-operation

To contribute, by appropriate means, to the development of contacts and co-operation in the various fields of culture, especially among creative artists and people engaged in cultural activities, in particular by making efforts to:

—promote for persons active in the field of culture, travel and meetings including, where necessary, those carried out on the basis of agreements, contracts or other special arrangements and which are relevant to their cultural co-operation;

—encourage in this way contacts among creative and performing artists and artistic groups with a view to their working together, making known their works in other participating States or exchanging views on topics relevant to their common activity;

—encourage, where necessary through appropriate arrangements, exchanges of trainees and specialists and the granting of scholarships for basic and advanced training in various fields of culture such as the arts and architecture, museums and libraries, literary studies and translation, and contribute to the creation of favourable conditions of reception in their respective institutions;

—encourage the exchange of experience in the training of organizers of cultural activities as well as of teachers and specialists in fields such as theatre, opera, ballet, music and fine arts;

—continue to encourage the organization of international meetings among creative artists, especially young creative artists, on current questions of artistic and literary creation which are of interest for joint study;

—study other possibilities for developing exchanges and co-operation among persons active in the field of culture, with a view to a better mutual knowledge of the cultural life of the participating States.

Fields and Forms of Co-operation

To encourage the search for new fields and forms of cultural co-operation, to these ends contributing to the conclusion among interested parties, where necessary, of appropriate agreements and arrangements, and in this context to promote:

—joint studies regarding cultural policies, in particular in their social aspects, and as they relate to planning, town-planning, educational and environmental policies, and the cultural aspects of tourism;

—the exchange of knowledge in the realm of cultural diversity, with a view to contributing thus to a better understanding by interested parties of such diversity where it occurs;

—the exchange of information, and as may be appropriate, meetings of experts, the elaboration and the execution of research programmes and projects, as well as their joint evaluation, and the dissemination of the results, on the subjects indicated above;

—such forms of cultural co-operation and the development of such joint projects as:

international events in the fields of the plastic and graphic arts, cinema, theatre, ballet, music, folklore, etc.; book fairs and exhibitions, joint performances of operatic and dramatic works, as well as performances given by soloists;

instrumental ensembles, orchestras, choirs and other artistic groups, including those composed of amateurs, paying due attention to the organization of international cultural youth events and the exchange of young artists;

the inclusion of works by writers and composers from the other participating States in the repertoires of soloists and artistic ensembles;

the preparation, translation and publication of articles, studies and monographs, as well as of low-cost books and of artistic and literary collections, suited to making better known respective cultural achievements, envisaging for this purpose meetings among experts and representatives of publishing houses;

the co-production and the exchange of films and of radio and television programmes, by promoting, in particular, meetings among producers, technicians and representatives of the public authorities with a view to working out favourable conditions for the execution of specific joint projects and by encouraging, in the field of co-production, the establishment of international filming teams;

the organization of competitions for architects and town-planners, bearing in mind the possible implementation of the best projects and the formation, where possible, of international teams;

the implementation of joint projects for conserving, restoring and showing to advantage works of art, historical and archaeological monuments and sites of cultural interest, with the help, in appropriate cases, of international organizations of a governmental or non-governmental character as well as of private institutions — competent and active in these fields — envisaging for this purpose:

> periodic meetings of experts of the interested parties to elaborate the necessary proposals, while bearing in mind the need to consider these questions in a wider social and economic context;

> the publication in appropriate periodicals of articles designed to make known and to compare, among the participating States, the most significant achievements and innovations;

> a joint study with a view to the improvement and possible harmonization of the different systems used to inventory and catalogue the historical monuments and places of cultural interest in their countries;

> the study of the possibilities for organizing international courses for the training of specialists in different disciplines relating to restoration.

* * *

National minorities or regional cultures. The participating States, recognizing the contribution that national minorities or regional cultures can make to co-operation among them in various fields of culture, intend, when such minorities or cultures exist within their territory, to facilitate this contribution, taking into account the legitimate interests of their members.

4. Co-operation and Exchanges in the Field of Education

The participating States,

Conscious that the development of relations of an international character in the fields of education and science contributes to a better mutual understanding and is to the advantage of all peoples as well as to the benefit of future generations,

Prepared to facilitate, between organizations, institutions and persons engaged in education and science, the further development of exchanges of knowledge and experience as well as of contacts, on the basis of special arrangements where these are necessary,

Desiring to strengthen the links among educational and scientific establishments and also to encourage their co-operation in sectors of common interest, particularly where the levels of knowledge and resources require efforts to be concerted internationally, and

Convinced that progress in these fields should be accompanied and supported by a wider knowledge of foreign languages,

Express to these ends their intention in particular:

(a) Extension of Relations

To expand and improve at the various levels co-operation and links in the fields of education and science, in particular by:

—concluding, where appropriate, bilateral or multilateral agreements providing for co-operation and exchanges among State institutions, non-governmental bodies and persons engaged in activities in education and science, bearing in mind the need both for flexibility and the fuller use of existing agreements and arrangements;

—promoting the conclusion of direct arrangements between universities and other institutions of higher education and research, in the framework of agreements between governments where appropriate;

—encouraging among persons engaged in education and science direct contacts and communications, including those based on special agreements or arrangements where these are appropriate.

(b) Access and Exchanges

To improve access, under mutually acceptable conditions, for students, teachers and scholars of the participating States to each other's educational, cultural and scientific institutions, and to intensify exchanges among these institutions in all areas of common interest, in particular by:

—increasing the exchange of information on facilities for study and courses open to foreign participants, as well as on the conditions under which they will be admitted and received;

—facilitating travel between the participating States by scholars, teachers and students for purposes of study, teaching and research as well as for improving knowledge of each other's educational, cultural and scientific achievements;

—encouraging the award of scholarships for study, teaching and research in their countries to scholars, teachers and students of other participating States;

—establishing, developing or encouraging programmes providing for the broader exchange of scholars, teachers and students, including the organization of symposia, seminars and collaborative projects, and the exchanges of educational and scholarly information such as university publications and materials from libraries;

—promoting the efficient implementation of such arrangements and programmes by providing scholars, teachers and students in good time with more detailed information about their placing in universities and institutes and the programmes envisaged for them; by granting them the opportunity to use relevant scholarly, scientific and open archival materials; and by facilitating their travel within the receiving State for the purpose of study or research as well as in the form of vacation tours on the basis of the usual procedures;

—promoting a more exact assessment of the problems of comparison and equivalence of academic degrees and diplomas by fostering the exchange of information on the organization, duration and content of studies, the comparison of methods of assessing levels of knowledge and academic qualifications, and, where feasible, arriving at the mutual recognition of academic degrees and diplomas either through governmental agreements, where necessary, or direct arrangements between universities and other institutions of higher learning and research,

—recommending, moreover, to the appropriate international organizations that they should intensify their efforts to reach a generally acceptable solution to the problems of comparison and equivalence between academic degrees and diplomas.

(c) Science

Within their competence to broaden and improve co-operation and exchanges in the field of science, in particular:

To increase, on a bilateral or multilateral basis, the exchange and dissemination of scientific information and documentation by such means as:

—making this information more widely available to scientists and research workers of the other participating States through, for instance, participation in international information-sharing programmes or through other appropriate arrangements;

—broadening and facilitating the exchange of samples and other scientific materials used particularly for fundamental research in the fields of natural sciences and medicine;

—inviting scientific institutions and universities to keep each other more fully and regularly informed about their current and contemplated research work in fields of common interest.

To facilitate the extension of communications and direct contacts between universities, scientific institutions and associations as well as among scientists and research workers, including those based where necessary on special agreements or arrangements, by such means as:

—further developing exchanges of scientists and research workers and encouraging the organization of preparatory meetings or working groups on research topics of common interest;

—encouraging the creation of joint teams of scientists to pursue research projects under arrangements made by the scientific institutions of several countries;

—assisting the organization and successful functioning of international conferences and seminars and participation in them by their scientists and research workers;

—furthermore envisaging, in the near future, a "Scientific Forum" in the form of a meeting of leading personalities in science from the participating States to discuss interrelated problems of common interest concerning current and future developments in science, and to promote the expansion of contacts, communications and the exchange of information between scientific institutions and among scientists;

—foreseeing, at an early date, a meeting of experts representing the participating States and their national scientific institutions, in order to prepare such a "Scientific Forum" in consultation with appropriate international organizations, such as UNESCO and the ECE;

—considering in due course what further steps might be taken with respect to the "Scientific Forum".

To develop in the field of scientific research, on a bilateral or multilateral basis, the co-ordination of programmes carried out in the participating States and the organization of joint programmes, especially in the areas mentioned below, which may involve the combined efforts of scientists and in certain cases the use of costly or unique equipment. The list of subjects in these areas is illustrative; and specific projects would have to be determined subsequently by the potential partners in the participating States, taking account of the contribution which could be made by appropriate international organizations and scientific institutions:

—*exact and natural sciences,* in particular fundamental research in such fields as mathematics, physics, theoretical physics, geophysics, chemistry, biology, ecology and astronomy;

—*medicine,* in particular basic research into cancer and cardiovascular diseases, studies on the diseases endemic in the developing countries, as well as medico-social research with special emphasis on occupational diseases, the rehabilitation of the handicapped and the care of mothers, children and the elderly;

—*the humanities and social sciences,* such as history, geography, philosophy, psychology, pedagogical research, linguistics, sociology, the legal, political and economic sciences; comparative studies on social, socio-economic and cultural phenomena which are of common interest to the participating States, especially the problems of human environment and urban development; and scientific studies on the methods of conserving and restoring monuments and works of art.

(d) Foreign Languages and Civilizations

To encourage the study of foreign languages and civilizations as an important means of expanding communication among peoples for their better acquaintance with the culture of each country, as well as for the strengthening of international co-operation; to this end to stimulate, within their competence, the further development and improvement of foreign language teaching and the diversification of choice of languages taught at various levels, paying due attention to less widely-spread or studied languages, and in particular:

—to intensify co-operation aimed at improving the teaching of foreign languages through exchanges of information and experience concerning the development and application of effective modern teaching methods and technical aids, adapted to the needs of different categories of students, including methods of accelerated teaching; and to consider the possibility of conducting, on a bilateral or multilateral basis, studies of new methods of foreign language teaching;

—to encourage co-operation between institutions concerned, on a bilateral or multilateral basis, aimed at exploiting more fully the resources of modern educational technology in language teaching, for example through comparative studies by their specialists and, where agreed, through exchanges or transfers of audio-visual materials, of materials used for preparing textbooks, as well as of information about new types of technical equipment used for teaching languages;

—to promote the exchange of information on the experience acquired in the training of language teachers and to intensify exchanges on a bilateral basis of language teachers and students as well as to facilitate their participation in summer courses in languages and civilizations, wherever these are organized;

—to encourage co-operation among experts in the field of lexicography with the aim of defining the necessary terminological equivalents, particularly in the scientific and technical disciplines, in order to facilitate relations among scientific institutions and specialists;

—to promote the wider spread of foreign language study among the different types of secondary education establishments and greater possibilities of choice between an increased number of European languages; and in this context to consider, wherever appropriate, the possibilities for developing the recruitment and training of teachers as well as the organization of the student groups required;

—to favour, in higher education, a wider choice in the languages offered to language students and greater opportunities for other students to study various foreign languages; also to facilitate, where desirable, the organization of courses in languages and civilizations, on the basis of special arrangements as necessary, to be given by foreign lecturers, particularly from European countries having less widely-spread or studied languages;

—to promote, within the framework of adult education, the further development of specialized programmes, adapted to various needs and interests, for teaching foreign languages to their own inhabitants and the languages of host countries to interested adults from other countries; in this context to encourage interested institutions to co-operate, for example, in the elaboration of programmes for teaching by radio and television and by accelerated methods, and also, where desirable, in the definition of study objectives for such programmes, with a view to arriving at comparable levels of language proficiency;

—to encourage the association, where appropriate, of the teaching of foreign languages with the study of the corresponding civilizations and also to make further efforts to stimulate interest in the study of foreign languages, including relevant out-of-class activities.

(e) Teaching Methods

To promote the exchange of experience, on a bilateral or multilateral basis, in teaching methods at all levels of education, including those used in permanent and adult education, as well as the exchange of teaching materials, in particular by:

—further developing various forms of contacts and co-operation in the different fields of pedagogical science, for example through comparative or joint studies carried out by interested institutions or through exchanges of information on the results of teaching experiments;

—intensifying exchanges of information on teaching methods used in various educational systems and on results of research into the processes by which pupils and students acquire knowledge, taking account of relevant experience in different types of specialized education;

—facilitating exchanges of experience concerning the organization and functioning of education intended for adults and recurrent education, the relationships between these and other forms and levels of education, as well as concerning the means of adapting education, including vocational and technical training, to the needs of economic and social development in their countries;

—encouraging exchanges of experience in the education of youth and adults in international understanding, with particular reference to those major problems of mankind whose solution calls for a common approach and wider international co-operation;

—encouraging exchanges of teaching materials—including school textbooks, having in mind the possibility of promoting mutual knowledge and facilitating the presentation of each country in such books—as well as exchanges of information on technical innovations in the field of education.

* * *

National minorities or regional cultures. The participating States, recognizing the contribution that national minorities or regional cultures can make to co-operation among them in various fields of education, intend, when such minorities or cultures exist within their territory, to facilitate this contribution, taking into account the legitimate interests of their members.

Follow-up to the Conference

The participating States,

Having considered and evaluated the progress made at the Conference on Security and Co-operation in Europe,

Considering further that, within the broader context of the world, the Conference is an important part of the process of improving security and developing co-operation in Europe and that its results will contribute significantly to this process,

Intending to implement the provisions of the Final Act of the Conference in order to give full effect to its results and thus to further the process of improving security and developing co-operation in Europe,

Convinced that, in order to achieve the aims sought by the Conference, they should make further unilateral, bilateral and multilateral efforts and continue, in the appropriate forms set forth below, the multilateral process initiated by the Conference,

1. *Declare their resolve,* in the period following the Conference, to pay due regard to and implement the provisions of the Final Act of the Conference;

(a) unilaterally in all cases which lend themselves to such action;

(b) bilaterally, by negotiations with other participating States;

(c) multilaterally, by meetings of experts of the participating States, and also within the framework of existing international organizations, such as the United Nations Economic Commission for Europe and UNESCO, with regard to educational, scientific and cultural co-operation;

2. *Declare furthermore their resolve* to continue the multilateral process initiated by the Conference;

(a) by proceeding to a thorough exchange of views both on the implementation of the provisions of the Final Act and of the tasks defined by the Conference, as well as, in the context of the questions dealt with by the latter, on the deepening of their mutual relations, the improvement of security and the development of co-operation in Europe, and the development of the process of détente in the future;

(b) by organizing to these ends meetings among their representatives, beginning with a meeting at the level of representatives appointed by the Ministers of Foreign Affairs. This meeting will define the appropriate modalities for the holding of other meetings which could include further similar meetings and the possibility of a new Conference;

3. The first of the meetings indicated above will be held at Belgrade in 1977. A preparatory meeting to organize this meeting will be held at Belgrade on 15 June 1977. The preparatory meeting will decide on the date, duration, agenda and other modalities of the meeting of representatives appointed by the Ministers of Foreign Affairs;

4. The rules of procedure, the working methods and the scale of distribution for the expenses of the Conference will, *mutatis mutandis,* be applied to the meetings envisaged in paragraphs 1 (c), 2 and 3 above. All the above-mentioned meetings will be held in the participating States in rotation. The services of a technical secretariat will be provided by the host country.

The original of this Final Act, drawn up in English, French, German, Italian, Russian and Spanish, will be transmitted to the Government of the Republic of Finland, which will retain it in its archives. Each of the participating States will receive from the Government of the Republic of Finland a true copy of this Final Act.

The text of this Final Act will be published in each participating State, which will disseminate it and make it known as widely as possible.

The Government of the Republic of Finland is requested to transmit to the Secretary-General of the United Nations the text of this Final Act, which is not eligible for registration under Article 102 of the Charter of the United Nations, with a view to its circulation to all the members of the Organization as an official document of the United Nations.

The Government of the Republic of Finland is also requested to transmit the text of this Final Act to the Director-General of UNESCO and to the Executive Secretary of the United Nations Economic Commission for Europe.

Wherefore, the undersigned High Representatives of the participating States, mindful of the high political significance which they attach to the results of the Conference, and declaring their determination to act in accordance with the provisions contained in the above texts, have subscribed their signatures below:

Done at Helsinki,
on 1st August
1975,
in the name of

Index

Index

About the Society

The American Society of International Law was organized in 1906 and incorported by special Act of Congress in 1950. Its objects are "to foster the study of international law and to promote the establishment and maintenance of international relations on the basis of law and justice."

Concerned with problems of international order and the legal framework for international relations for almost three quarters of a century, the Society serves as a meeting place, forum and collegial research center for scholars, officials, practicing lawyers, students, and others. The Society is hospitable to all viewpoints in its meetings and in its publications. Those publications include the leading periodicals, *The American Journal of International Law* and *International Legal Materials*. In addition, the Society publishes books, reports, and the occasional paper series, *Studies in Transnational Legal Policy,* produced by an extensive Research and Study Program under the supervision of its Board of Review and Development.

The Society's membership, which exceeds 5000, is drawn from some 100 countries. Membership is open to all, whatever their nationality or profession.

About the Authors

THOMAS BUERGENTHAL is Fulbright and Jaworski Professor of Law at the University of Texas School of Law.

SUZANNE BASTID is Professor of the University of Law, Economics, and Social Sciences, University of Paris II.

ANTONIO CASSESE is Professor of International Organization at the University of Florence; he is also a member of the U.N. Sub-Commission on Prevention of Discrimination and Protection of Minorities.

GÉRARD COHEN JONATHAN is Dean of the Faculty of Law and Political Science of the University of Strasbourg.

JOCHEN ABR. FROWEIN is a member of the faculty of the University of Bielefeld.

LOUIS HENKIN is Professor of Law, Columbia University School of Law.

JEAN PAUL JACQUÉ is a member of the Faculty of Law and Political Science of the University of Strasbourg.

VIRGINIA A. LEARY is Associate Professor of Law at the State University of New York School of Law.